KOSOVO IN A NUTSHELL

A Brief History and Chronology of Events

Robert Elsie

Centre for Albanian Studies, London

Publisher's Cataloging-in-Publication data

Elsie, Robert, 1950-
    Kosovo in a nutshell : a brief history and chronology of
events / Robert Elsie.
    121 p. cm.
    ISBN 978-1508496748
    Series : Albanian studies.
    Includes bibliographical references.

1. Kosovo (Republic). 2. Kosovo (Republic) --History. 3.
Albania --History. I. Title. II. Series.

DR2076 .E47 2015
949.7/1 --dc23

Albanian Studies, Vol. 6
ISBN 978-1508496748

The material in this book was first published in good part as the
introduction to: Robert Elsie, *Historical Dictionary of Kosovo*,
second edition (Lanham, Toronto, Plymouth: Scarecrow Press,
2010).

Cover photo: View of Gjakova (photo: Robert Elsie, April
2010).

Table of Contents

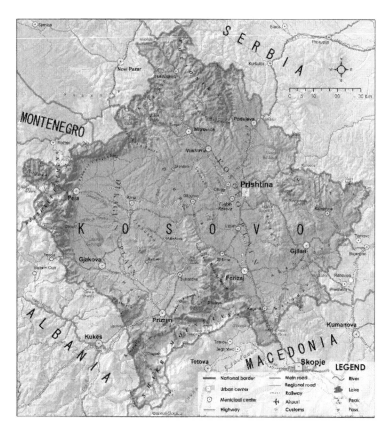

Map of Kosovo, by Ismail Gagica, 2015

Kosovo: An Emerging European Nation

Kosovo is the newest country in Europe. It is the seventh and probably last state to arise from the ruins of former Yugoslavia. It is also one of the poorest countries in Europe. Kosovo's long struggle for identity, self-determination and independence has been bitter, and it will be in need of international assistance for a while before it can become a normal European nation like the others.

For centuries, Kosovo, also known as Kosova, was part of the Ottoman Empire, and for most of the 20th century, it was a province of what was once Yugoslavia. After the military conflict in 1998-1999 and a period of administration by the United Nations, Kosovo declared its independence from Serbia on 17 February 2008.

Land and People

Kosovo is situated in the southern interior of the Balkan Peninsula in southeastern Europe, between 43°16' and 41°47' degrees of latitude north, and 20°00' and 21°47' degrees of longitude east. It is a landlocked, square-shaped country of 10,877 square kilometres, about the size of Montenegro, Northern Ireland or the U.S. state of Connecticut. Kosovo's surface area is less than half of that of Albania, having a north-south distance of about 147 and an east-west distance of about 152 kilometres. The country borders on the Republic of Albania to the west, the Republic of Montenegro to the northwest, the Republic of Serbia to the north and east and the Republic of Macedonia to the south.

Natural barriers are formed by the northern Albanian Alps to the west, along the border with Albania, and by the Sharr mountain range to the south along the border with Macedonia, whereas the northern and eastern borders with Serbia consist in good part of low mountains and rolling hills. The highest peak in Kosovo, Mount Gjeravica, has an elevation of 2,656 meters.

Over half of the surface of Kosovo is arable land and more than a third of it is forest. The climate is conducive to agriculture, the soil is of generally good quality and there is sufficient water from the many rivers and streams. The major rivers of Kosovo are the White Drin (Alb. Drini i Bardhë, BCS Beli Drim), that flows through Albania into the Adriatic; the Sitnica and Ibër (BCS Ibar) that flow through Serbia into the Black Sea; and the Lepenc (BCS Lepenac), that flows through Macedonia into the Aegean Sea.

Settlements in Kosovo are concentrated primarily on two central plateaux stretching in a north-south direction. The eastern part of Kosovo, known geographically at the Plain of Kosovo (Alb. Fusha e Kosovës, BCS Kosovo Polje), is a plateau running from Mitrovica southwards past Prishtina and Ferizaj almost to Kaçanik. It has an elevation of 500-600 meters. Western Kosovo, known geographically as the Dukagjin Plateau or Metohija (Alb.

Rrafshi i Dukagjinit, BCS Metohija), is a plateau running from Istog and Peja in the north down to Prizren in the south. It has an elevation of 300-500 meters.

Kosovo has a population of some two million people, roughly equivalent to that of Macedonia or Slovenia. It is inhabited primarily (to 92 percent) by Albanians, the same Indo-European people as in the neighbouring Republic of Albania. There are also minorities of Serbs, Bosniacs, Roma and Turks. The Serbs, though now only five percent of the population, played an important role in Kosovo's history and held political power throughout most of the 20th century. The main languages spoken in Kosovo, accordingly, are Albanian, used by about 92 percent of the population, and BCS (Bosnian-Croatian-Serbian), commonly known here as Serbian, used by about six percent of the population. English and German are the best-known foreign languages.

The name Kosovo, from BCS *kos* "blackbird" with a Slavic *-ovo* adjectival suffix, seems to have been first used in connection with the historic Battle of Kosovo that was fought in 1389 on the "plain of the blackbirds."

History

Kosovo has fixed and recognized borders, but until 2008 it never constituted an independent state of its own. In the first millennium A.D., it was part of the Roman Empire and later fell to Byzantium. In the period 1184-1216, it came under the rule of the Serb Nemanja dynasty from neighbouring Rascia (Raška) and formed an integral part of the medieval Serb Empire. The famed Battle of Kosovo of 1389 marked the beginning of Ottoman expansion into Kosovo. By the year 1455, all of the country was under Turkish rule and was to remain under the sway of the sultans until the early years of the 20th century.

The late 19th century saw the rise of the Albanian nationalist movement that crystallized in the League of Prizren in 1878. This League took over Kosovo and governed it until 1881, when it was quashed by Ottoman troops. From that time until the end of Ottoman rule, or better misrule, uprisings in Kosovo were a matter of course. Yet the Albanians, who were by this time the majority of the population, were hesitant to cut all ties with the Ottoman Empire for fear that Serbia might invade and take over the country. In October 1912, this is exactly what happened.

Kosovo under Serb Rule

As the Ottoman Empire crumbled, leaving Kosovo in a state of anarchy, the Serb army under King Peter invaded from the north and occupied all of Kosovo. Hideous massacres, recorded in the chronicle *Albaniens Golgatha* (Albania's Golgotha), Vienna 1913, by Austrian Socialist Leo Freundlich, were committed against the Albanian population. Village after village was razed to the ground, with the inhabitants being bayoneted or burned alive. The Serbs of Kosovo, for their part, welcomed the army of King Peter as liberators, and liberated they were.

The Conference of Ambassadors, meeting in London from December 1912 to August 1913 to discuss events in the Balkans, confirmed the independence of Albania itself, but agreed to recognize Serb rule over Kosovo, thus excluding 40 percent of the Albanian population in the Balkans from Albania itself. It was a tragic mistake that haunted the Balkans right to the end of the 20th century.

Kosovo was under Serb rule for over 80 years, throughout which, from start to finish, it had a large Albanian majority population. The people of Kosovo were never consulted as to whether they wished to be part of Serbia, and they did not. Had there been a free and democratic referendum on Serb rule at any time from the military invasion of 1912 to the withdrawal of Serb forces in 1999, the population of Kosovo, in its overwhelming majority, would undoubtedly have said "no, thank you." Thus, although the inclusion of Kosovo in Serbia and Yugoslavia was largely recognized internationally, it lacked basic democratic legitimacy. As a consequence of this, although regimes in Belgrade changed over the decades (royalist, communist, democratic), one constant factor was dictatorship, and often military dictatorship in Kosovo. It could never be otherwise because anything Belgrade had to offer was fundamentally against the wishes of the people of Kosovo. Vociferous claims emanating from Belgrade that Kosovo was "part of Serbia" were not unlike protests in France in the 1950s that Algeria was not a colony but "part of France." In neither case were the people of the territory in question ever consulted.

The history of the Kosovo Albanians from the beginning of Serb rule in 1912 to its very end in June 1999 is one of tragedy and unspeakable injustice. Had there been any semblance of national and minority rights for non-Slavs in the new Kingdom of the Serbs, Croats and Slovenes, things might have been different. The Kosovo Albanians, as non-Slavs and as Muslims in their majority, were looked upon from the start with great suspicion and were deprived of basic rights. Books and school education in Albanian remained as illegal as they had been under Ottoman rule, and very few Albanians ever gained positions in government administration.

The 1920s saw the rise of official Yugoslav government campaigns, some of them very violent, to depopulate Kosovo of its original inhabitants and to colonize it with peasants and farmers from Serbia and the Vojvodina. In September 1920, a "decree on the colonization of the new southern lands" facilitated the takeover by Serb colonists of large Ottoman estates and of land seized from Albanian rebels. By 1925, the government colonization programme, which had brought some 70,000 colonists to Kosovo, equivalent to about 10 percent of the total population, had raised the proportion of Serbs there from 24 percent in 1919 to 38 percent. In June 1931, a new Yugoslav law "on the colonization of the southern regions" entered into force and, in 1933, the Yugoslav government began negotiations with the Turkish government for the deportation of the Muslim population to Turkey. By 1935, an orchestrated wave of confiscation of land from Albanians was well underway. The culmination of prewar projects for the ethnic cleansing of Kosovo can be seen in a chilling paper presented to the Serb Academy of Sciences in Belgrade on 7 March 1937. Its author, Vaso Čubrilović, a noted Serb scholar and political figure of the age, called for nothing less than the expulsion of all Albanians from their native Kosovo. By 1939, there were about 60,000 Slav colonists in Kosovo, equivalent to 9.3 percent of the population.

It is no wonder therefore that Kosovo Albanian sympathies were divided at the time of the Axis invasion of Yugoslavia in 1941. Although there was no particular enthusiasm for the new Axis administration, most Kosovo Albanians found it preferable to Serb rule. In the autumn of 1941, Italian forces occupied and annexed most of Kosovo, which, under Benito Mussolini, was finally, though briefly, reunited with Albania. It was during the Italian and German occupation that the tables turned for the Serb and Montenegrin colonists in Kosovo, who, for the most part, were driven back out of the country, not without terror and violence. An estimated 20,000 Serbs and Montenegrins fled for their lives in the spring and summer of 1941, many being deported to forced labour camps or to work in the Trepça mines. Kosovo Albanian historians assert that the Albanians drove out only the new settlers and colonists who had earlier taken their land, and, generally, did not attack the traditional Kosovo Serb communities whom they regarded as their neighbours. In 1943-1944, however, under the Albanian nationalist Second League of Prizren, there was general terror against the Serbs and Montenegrins, and about 40,000 of them had been driven out of the country.

Fascist rule and the reunification of Kosovo with Albania were short-lived. By the end of November 1944, all of Kosovo had fallen into the hands of the victorious Yugoslav partisans, and had been returned to Serb administration. Tito's communists originally promised to let the people of Kosovo decide democratically as to whether they wished to be part of Albania or of Yugoslavia. Tito, however, soon reneged on his promise, realizing that the so-called "Marxist solution" to the Kosovo question would never be accepted by Serbia. Kosovo was thus incorporated into socialist Yugoslavia against its will, under the law of 3 September 1945. It was, nonetheless, recognized as an "autonomous region."

Relations with neighbouring communist Albania under Enver Hoxha were initially very good, but by 1949, in the early years of the Cold War, they reached an all-time low. In order to keep power and to counterbalance Yugoslav influence in his tiny and impoverished country, Hoxha aligned Albania with Stalinist Russia. Claims on Kosovo would only have destabilized his rule. The border between Albania and Kosovo was thus closed and became as impervious as any communist border could be. Even in the mid-1990s, long after the fall of communism in both countries, Kosovo Albanians still required special exit visas to visit Albania, which were usually denied.

Yugoslav communism brought the Kosovo Albanians a modicum of rights as citizens, but as an ethnic group they were still deprived of full equality. Particularly difficult were the years of Aleksandar Ranković (1909-1984). As Tito's right-hand man, Ranković was initially Serb minister of the interior and, from 1953-1966, was deputy prime minister. He despised and mistrusted the Albanians and made sure that his police and security forces kept them under strict control. The infamous and ludicrous campaign for the collection of arms in 1956 was so rigorous that Albanian families, faced with savage beatings and prison, were forced to buy weapons (from the Serb police) in order to give them up (to the Serb police). The whole country breathed a sigh of relief when Ranković was purged in 1966.

The Brioni Plenum of July 1966 marked the beginning of a substantial improvement in the lot of the Kosovo Albanians. In March 1967, Tito paid a visit to Kosovo. In 1969, official usage of the pejorative term for the Albanians, *šiptar*, was banned in favour of the neutral term *albanac*.

The founding of the University of Prishtina in February 1970 gave the Kosovo Albanians something essential that they had always been denied: access to higher education in their own language. Within one short decade, a new elite of professors, doctors, lawyers and educated political figures arose to give leadership and direction to the country for the first time.

In February 1974, the new constitutions of Yugoslavia, Serbia and Kosovo accorded the autonomous province a status virtually equal to that of the republics in the Yugoslav federation. Though still under Serb tutelage, Kosovo could now manage most of its own affairs. It had its own parliament, its own police force and its own national bank. Run by local Albanian communists, Kosovo was equally represented with the six republics and the Vojvodina in the federal presidency. And the Albanians won the right to fly their own national flag.

In many ways, the period from 1967 to 1981 marked a "golden age" in the history of Kosovo. There was a semblance of equality among all citizens, and a nascent spirit of fraternity showed that Albanians and Serbs could indeed live together. After years of nationalist contestation, the two communities began to work together for a common good. Economically, however, Kosovo made little progress and this, in the long run, proved to be its downfall. Despite its rich mineral resources, it remained by far the poorest and most underdeveloped region of Yugoslavia. In 1979, it had an average per capita income of 795 U.S. dollars, as compared to the Yugoslav average of $2,635 and to $5,315 in Slovenia.

The initially peaceful protests of March and April 1981 and the brutality of their suppression by the Belgrade authorities brought this "golden age" to a definitive close. What began as student demonstrations at the University of Prishtina to protest against miserable living and studying conditions soon transformed themselves into a political movement for republic status and absolute equality with the other parts of the Yugoslav federation. Kosovo had always been denied the status of a republic because this would have given it the legal right to secede from the federation, something to which the Serbs were fanatically opposed. Belgrade dubbed the unrest "counter-revolutionary" and imposed a state of siege. The troubles, which spread throughout Kosovo as an uprising against Serb rule, were swiftly and brutally squashed when the federal police and the army were brought in from Serbia and elsewhere. Thousands of Albanians, apprehended in mainly peaceful demonstrations, were sentenced to long years of prison for counter-revolutionary and separatist activity. The people of Kosovo were in shock. So was Yugoslavia.

The year 1981 marked the beginning of the gradual Serb takeover of Kosovo. The situation for the Kosovo Albanians got worse every year throughout the 1980s. The population grew sullen and angry, and tried its best simply to ignore the Serb state. The people knew that they were powerless to oppose the might of Belgrade.

In the autumn of 1988, after several years of silence and withdrawal, there were once again major demonstrations against Serb rule, this time when Slobodan Milošević dismissed Albanian political leaders without the endorsement of the local communist party. On 18 November, factory workers, students and children joined the miners of Trepça in a 100,000-strong peaceful march on Prishtina. In February of the following year, the miners went on a widely publicized hunger strike that shook the population to its core. The protest movement was again put down by force, and thousands of people were arrested. In April, in Ferizaj alone, over 1,000 workers were put on trial.

Belgrade showed no intention or interest in settling Kosovar grievances. On the contrary, the Serb leadership decided to resolve the Kosovo question by openly depriving the Albanians of their economic existence, i.e., by starving them out and forcing them to emigrate. A process of "differentiation" was introduced, by which tens of thousands of Albanians lost their jobs and livelihood. Virtually all Albanians were fired from management and government positions under the pretence that they were not loyal to the Serb state, and indeed, they were not. Deprived of their jobs, many of them had no choice but to

15

flee abroad in search of work in Germany and Switzerland. Belgrade had reverted to the strategy it had used successfully in the 1930s: ethnic cleansing, though in the 1980s still in a discreet form. With hundreds of thousands of Kosovo Albanians seeking refuge abroad, the international community now began to take note of the Kosovo question for the first time.

On 28 March 1989, the parliament in Belgrade for all practical purposes rescinded the autonomy status of Kosovo. The population was once again in shock. By June, when Slobodan Milošević fuelled the nationalist sentiments of the Serb minority with his speech at Gazimestan near Prishtina to commemorate the 600th anniversary of the Battle of Kosovo, the country was on the verge of civil war.

Events of 1990 made it evident to everyone that there was no turning back from the brink. In March of that year, the Serb parliament invoked the infamous "Programme for the Attainment of Peace, Freedom and Prosperity in the Socialist Autonomous Province of Kosovo," which provided financial assistance to Kosovo Serbs and forced even more Kosovo Albanians to leave the country. The screws were turned and the pressure mounted.

In April and May 1990, thousands of Albanian school children were taken to hospital suffering from stomach pains, headaches and nausea. The Serb authorities spoke of mass hysteria, whereas the Albanian population suspected poisoning. Indeed, subsequent analyses carried out by a United Nations (UN) expert on toxicology revealed the presence in the children's blood and urine samples of the toxic substances Sarin and Tabun, which were being manufactured and utilized by the Yugoslav army at the time for chemical weapons. In May 1990, an amendment to the Serb law on universities made the use of "minority languages," i.e., Albanian, illegal at institutions of higher education in Kosovo. On 26 June, most provincial competencies were then taken over "temporarily" by Serb government and administrative authorities by virtue of a new law on the "Activities of the Institutions of the Republic under Exceptional Circumstances."

Finally, in July 1990, Serb forces intervened physically by breaking up and abolishing the parliament and the government of Kosovo. They also shut down all Albanian-language media. There was no more semblance of representative government, no more radio, no more television, not even a daily newspaper. In the autumn of that year, the authorities then closed down virtually all Albanian-language schools and educational institutions, firing teachers and professors. Some 1,835 doctors and nurses were also expelled from hospitals and medical facilities, many of them forcibly.

The Kosovo Albanians were aware that they were outnumbered, and outgunned. There could be no course of action but passive resistance, a political strategy propagated from the start by their leader Ibrahim Rugova. With time, under the Democratic League of Kosovo, they created their own parallel state structures, including a government (in exile), a state president, a parliament, schools and a modicum of social assistance for the population, supported primarily by the three-percent tax paid by Kosovo Albanian workers abroad.

On 2 July 1990, 114 of the 123 members of the parliament of Kosovo, meeting in the street outside their locked assembly building, declared Kosovo to be an "equal and independent entity within the framework of the Yugoslav federation," i.e., a Yugoslav "Republic of Kosovo." On 7 September of that year, at a secret assembly in Kaçanik, they promulgated a new constitution for the Republic of Kosovo. Kosovo was to be a sovereign state among the other nations of Yugoslavia. A year later, on 22 September 1991, this parliament proclaimed the independence of the "Republic of Kosovo." In a national referendum held on the issue on 26-30 September 1991, 99.86 percent of voters (with an 87.01 percent turnout) approved the move. An official government in exile was set up in Germany under Prime Minister Bujar Bukoshi and, in May 1992, Ibrahim Rugova, still living in Prishtina, was elected president of the unrecognized and thus essentially fictive state.

In the following years, international mediators pleaded with the Kosovo Albanians to avoid any further escalation of the conflict, and promised to address their grievances as soon as the Bosnia conflict was under control. However, Kosovo was excluded from the Dayton Agreement of November 1995, and no international mediators returned to Prishtina to fulfil their promises.

Between 1993 and 1998, the level of oppression exerted on the Kosovo Albanians was unprecedented in Europe since the Nazi period. With no solution in sight, it was only a matter of time before organized armed resistance became a reality. The population realized increasingly that the long years of passive resistance under Ibrahim Rugova had led them nowhere. In April 1996, the underground Kosovo Liberation Army (KLA), founded in December 1993, began carrying out coordinated attacks on persons representing and collaborating with the Serb state. It made its first public appearance at a funeral in Drenica on 28 November 1997 and soon enjoyed massive support.

The Kosovo War broke out in the early months of 1998, when Serb troops began a major offensive in the Drenica region, attacking the villages of Çirez and Likoshana. Soon thereafter, the Kosovo Liberation Army issued a communiqué calling on all Albanians to join the fight against the Serb regime. By the end of May, one-fourth of the territory of Kosovo was a war zone, and much of it was under KLA control. Militarily, the KLA and the local population initially did quite well in combating Serb forces. In the summer of 1998, however, a new Serb offensive reversed the Albanian gains of the spring, and by October, the KLA was in disarray and agreed to a cease-fire. Despite this, fighting continued and intensified throughout the winter.

Kosovo first received major international attention in January 1999 with the discovery, by a delegation of the Organization for Security and Cooperation in Europe (OSCE) under William Walker, of the bodies of 45 Albanian civilians in Reçak (BCS Račak), massacred by the Serb police. Last-minute peace talks were held in France in February and March, but to no avail. The Serb side refused to sign the peace accord, thus making intervention by the North Atlantic Treaty Organization (NATO) inevitable.

NATO forces began their bombing campaign over Yugoslavia on 24 March 1999. In revenge, the Belgrade authorities launched a well-prepared and well-orchestrated campaign to "cleanse" Kosovo of all of its Albanian population. Over half a million people were put to flight, most of them being expelled or taking refuge in Albania and Macedonia. The NATO bombing campaign lasted until mid-June 1999 when the parliament in Belgrade finally agreed to withdraw Serb forces from Kosovo. Serb rule had come to an end.

Kosovo under United Nations Administration

In early July 1999, the Organization for Security and Co-operation in Europe sets up a mission in Kosovo to be known as the United Nations Interim Administrative Mission in Kosovo (UNMIK), and French politician Bernard Kouchner was appointed as Special Representative of the UN Secretary-General to oversee the new administration. By August, 850,000 Albanian refugees had returned to Kosovo, and about half of the Kosovo Serb population, some 100,000 people, had fled to Serbia. A transitional council of representatives of all ethnic communities, including the remaining Serbs, was called together in August. By the autumn of 1999, political parties had been formed, and an Interim Administrative Council began to function in early 2000. On 28 October 2000, local elections were held, the first free elections in Kosovo's history. The majority of the populace voted for the Democratic League of Kosovo (LDK) under Ibrahim Rugova. Parliamentary elections followed a year later, on 17 November 2001, with the LDK once again the leading party, but without an absolute majority.

Parliamentary life thus resumed on 10 December 2001 with the first session of the new Kosovo Assembly. On 28 February 2002, Bajram Rexhepi was elected prime minister, and Ibrahim Rugova subsequently assumed the title of head of state. A new multi-ethnic Kosovo Police service was created, and the KLA was demobilized and transformed into the Kosovo Protection Corps. Thereafter, UNMIK gradually began transferring most of its administrative competencies in Kosovo to the elected government authorities.

A sudden outbreak of ethnic rioting and anti-Serb violence occurred in mid-March 2004, the worst since the Kosovo War. The events, sparked by a series of relatively minor incidents and inaccurate media reporting, subsided almost as quickly as they arose, but they left in their wake shock and much destruction, in particular of Serb homes and churches. The initially unchecked rioting proved just how fragile the reconciliation progress was, and how ineffective KFOR was in ensuring public order.

The parliamentary elections of October 2004 were held under the supervision of the new central electoral commission. They resulted in a coalition between the LDK and the Alliance for the Future of Kosovo (AAK), making Ramush Haradinaj prime minister. Haradinaj, a former hardline KLA leader, did much for the Serb community and promoted reconciliation, but he was forced to resign in March 2005 when he was indicted for war crimes by the International Criminal Court for the former Yugoslavia (ICTY) in The Hague. After a lengthy trial, he was acquitted of all charges. Haradinaj was followed in office by Bajram Kosumi of the AAK who resigned the following year, in March 2006, and was replaced by another former KLA commander, Agim Çeku. The year 2006 also marked the death of President Ibrahim Rugova, who was succeeded as head of state by Fatmir Sejdiu.

The Road to Independence

The burning question for most people in Kosovo during the years of international administration was the country's final status. United Nations Security Council Resolution 1244, adopted on 10 June 1999 at the end of the Kosovo War to provide for a legal international presence in the country after the withdrawal of Serb forces, set forth that there would be a political process to determine Kosovo's final status, taking into account the Rambouillet accords. The United Nations and the international community had long not been willing or able to come to terms with the issue of final status and endeavored to postpone any discussion of it as much as possible. In April 2002, Special Representative Michael Steiner launched the slogan "Standards before Status" to try to convince the population of Kosovo that there was no sense in addressing the status issue until certain standards had been achieved. Steiner's objective was both to postpone a thorny discussion of Kosovo's status and, at the same time, to prepare Kosovo as a functioning democracy with respect for minority rights and an operating market economy to meet future requirements for independence and/or for membership in the European Union (EU).

In 2005, Norwegian envoy Kai Eide reported to the United Nations that there was no advantage to be gained by stalling the status process. In November of that year, when a Contact Group (France, Germany, Italy, Russia, the United Kingdom and the United States) had set forth the 'guiding principles' of status resolution, i.e., that there would be no return to the situation before 1999 and that there would be no change in Kosovo's borders, i.e., no partition of Kosovo or union with a neighbouring state, and had agreed that any future status would have to be acceptable to the people of Kosovo, UN Secretary-General Kofi Annan appointed the former president of Finland, Martti Ahtisaari, as his special representative to lead the status process. Ahtisaari brought Prishtina and Belgrade together for further negotiations on practical issues and on the status question, and then drafted a comprehensive proposal for status resolution. The so-called Ahtisaari Plan recommended independence, subject to a period of international supervision under an International Civilian Office (ICO). Prishtina accepted the proposal, but Belgrade rejected it.

On 3 April 2007, Martti Ahtisaari submitted his plan to the United Nations Security Council for approval. Due to Russian opposition, however, the Security Council was not able to reach agreement on it, and yet further negotiations were recommended, this time under the auspices of a 'Troika' (EU, Russia U.S.) which was to report to the secretary-general in December 2007. After intense negotiations held in Baden, near Vienna, the

Troika reported the obvious, that it was not possible to find a mutually acceptable agreement.

Meanwhile, parliamentary elections had been held once again in November 2007 and resulted in a victory for the Democratic Party of Kosovo (PDK) under the new prime minister, Hashim Thaçi. The Serb minority largely boycotted these elections.

On 17 February 2008, Kosovo declared its independence from Serbia and, at the same time, committed itself to respecting its obligations under the Ahtisaari Plan, to embracing multi-ethnicity as a fundamental principle of good governance, and to welcoming a period of international supervision. Most western countries and most members of the European Union recognized Kosovo shortly after the declaration, and the Dutch diplomat Pieter Feith was appointed as the first International Civilian Representative (ICR) and European Union Special Representative (EUSR) to Kosovo. The EU also agreed upon a European Union Rule of Law Mission (EULEX) to oversee police work and judicial affairs.

In line with the Ahtisaari Plan, the government of Kosovo enacted laws on minority protection, decentralization, special protection zones for Serb cultural and religious sites, local self-government and new municipal boundaries. Parliament also approved a new constitution which entered into force on 15 June 2008, having been certified by the ICR as a modern constitution that "provides comprehensive rights for members of communities as well as effective guarantees for the protection of the national, linguistic and religious identity of all communities."

In December 2008, EULEX reached its initial operative capacity with the deployment of over 1,000 international police officers, judges, prosecutors and customs officers. At the same time, UNMIK substantially scaled back its presence. It was initially foreseen that UNMIK would withdraw from Kosovo upon the arrival of EULEX, but Russia opposed this. By April 2009, EULEX had achieved full operational capacity. In June 2009, Kosovo joined the International Monetary Fund and the World Bank, a step that finally enables it to acquire much-needed external capital in the form of grants, emergency financing and project funding.

Quo Vadis, Kosovo?

After almost nine decades of misrule under Serbia and almost a decade of United Nations administration and unclarified status, Kosovo is now the newest country in Europe. According to surveys taken in the year of independence, it had the youngest and most optimistic population on the continent. The declaration of independence in February 2008 was a moment of pride and joy for the Kosovo Albanians and most other ethnic communities, although it was, admittedly, also one of great apprehension for the Kosovo Serb minority. Reconciliation will take time, and independence is only one step in an arduous process of nation-building. The new Republic of Kosovo still faces substantial challenges and will need to rely to a large extent on the support of the

European Union and the international community for many years to come.

Among the major problems Kosovo is confronted with is the economy. As one of the poorest countries in Europe (only Moldova is poorer), Kosovo imports great quantities of goods and services but exports by comparison very little. Its catastrophic balance of payments is only kept in keel by international support and financial remittances from Kosovars living abroad. About 35 percent of its citizens live below the poverty line and about 15 percent live in extreme poverty.

Secondly, the Kosovo Serbs, only five or six percent of the population, but still very influential, do not identify with the new State in which they live and continue to look to Serbia as their only country. The result of this stance is that the Government of Kosovo does not have effective control over all of its territory. The much-lauded and unquestionably needed Ahtisaari Plan in fact only served to reinforce the division of the country.

Thirdly are Kosovo's tenuous relations with the neighbouring, and much larger Republic of Serbia. Although it accepted the independence of Montenegro with little opposition, Serbia has not taken kindly to the independence of Kosovo. The Belgrade government bitterly opposed the "unilateral" declaration, but had no alternative to propose that would have been acceptable to the people of Kosovo. Emotionally, most Serbs still regarded Kosovo as theirs and theirs alone, and there was anti-Western rioting in Belgrade when leading Western countries recognized Kosovo's independence. The declaration was controversial on the international scene as well. Most Western countries recognized Kosovo within a couple of months of the act, but some, such as Russia, threw their support behind Serbia. Even within the European Union there was no unanimity, and a few EU member states - with minority problems of their own - have withheld recognition.

Finally, Kosovo also has a substantial image problem. Its name has conjured up images of ethnic conflict, eternal political crisis and organized crime. It has been decried in the press and in some international reports as a mafia state and as a haven for drug traffickers and criminals. While it is undeniable that crime and corruption exist in Kosovo, as they do in most countries with a similar level of economic development, the rampant human trafficking and unchecked organized crime that flourished in the early years of the UNMIK administration have been largely dampened.

Kosovo is, in fact, a very safe country to visit. According to a report of the Kosovo Stability Initiative, the murder rate is about the same as in Sweden and there are more police officers per capita than in Singapore. By comparison, Northern Ireland has 960 percent more violent crimes and there are almost four times more firearms per capita in Finland than in Kosovo. Despite this, much remains to be done to consolidate structures and to improve the country's image.

At the time of her surreptitious journey to Ottoman Kosovo in 1908, the intrepid English traveller Edith Durham wrote: "There is a joy that never palls the first glimpse into the unknown land. On the other side of the pass, a magnificent valley lay below us, thickly wooded with beech, and beyond were the lands which two rival races each claim as their birthright - one of the least-known corners of Europe." Kosovo has long been the meeting place between the two "rival races," the interface between Albanian and Serbian worlds, and this confrontation has indeed often - though not always - been a source of irritation. The country's dual identity is now being overlaid by a strong European dimension. If Kosovo and the other countries of southeastern Europe can be swiftly assisted towards integration and membership in the European Union, sovereignty and border issues will fade and soon become irrelevant. The former president of Germany, Roman Herzog, once said on a visit to the southern Balkans, "Let us keep the borders where they are, but let us stamp them into the ground so that no one can see them." The day will soon dawn, it is to be hoped, when the political and emotional borders that separate Albania, Kosovo and Serbia will be no more significant than those between France, Belgium and the Netherlands. The often sombre past will be nothing more than... the past.

Robert Elsie
Berlin, Germany

Chronology of Events

Early Kosovo (to 1450)

547-548
Slavic invasion and settlement of Kosovo.

ca. 850
The first Bulgarian Empire seizes Kosovo from the Byzantine Empire.

1014-1018
Restoration of Byzantine rule.

1184-1196
Serb expansion from Rascia (Raška) into eastern Kosovo under Stefan Nemanja I.

ca. 1208
Stefan Nemanja II of Rascia conquers most of western Kosovo.

1216
With the final conquest of Prizren, all of Kosovo is brought under Serb rule.

1219

Sava Nemanja (Saint Sava), brother of Stefan Nemanja II, establishes an autocephalic Serbian Orthodox Church and expels Greek bishops from Kosovo.

1252

The Patriarchate of the Serbian Orthodox Church is established in Peja (Peć).

1330

Foundation of the monastery of Deçan.

1346

The Orthodox archbishop of Peja assumes the title of patriarch.

1389

15 June (28 June old style): The Battle of Kosovo brings a gradual end to Serb rule in Kosovo.

1396

Turkish garrisons and elements of an Ottoman administration are set up in some parts of Kosovo.

1405

Birth of Scanderbeg.

1409

War in Kosovo between Stefan Lazarević and his brother, the latter supported by Sultan Suleyman.

1423

Presence of an Ottoman court of law in Prishtina.

1427

Djuradj Branković succeeds his uncle Stefan Lazarević as ruler of Kosovo as part of a larger Serbian territory under Ottoman vassalage.

1443-1468

Uprising of Scanderbeg in Albania.

1448

17-19 October: Second Battle of Kosovo that pitted the army of Hungarian commander János Hunyadi against a larger Ottoman force. After three days of fighting, Hunyadi and his Hungarian army were forced to flee.

Kosovo under Ottoman Rule (to 1912)

1455

All of Kosovo is brought under Ottoman control. **1 June:** The rich mining town of Novobërda surrenders to Ottoman forces under Sultan Mehmet II after a 40-day siege. Three hundred twenty youths of the town are taken away to join the Janissaries, and the women are "distributed among the heathens." **21 June:** Prizren surrenders to Ottoman forces.

1461

Construction of the Fatih Mosque in Prishtina.

1468

17 January: Death of Scanderbeg.

1557
Restoration of the Serbian Orthodox Patriarchate in Peja by Ottoman vizier Mehmed Pasha Sokolović.

1593-1606
War between the Habsburgs and the Ottoman Empire.

1660
Turkish traveler Evliya Çelebi journeys through Kosovo.

1683-1699
War between the Habsburgs and the Ottoman Empire.

1685
Albanian-language *Cuneus Prophetarum* is published in Padua by Pjetër Bogdani, native of Guri i Hasit near Prizren.

1689
Autumn: A small Habsburg army under Count Eneo Piccolomini conquers Kosovo and establishes Austrian control over the whole area.

1690
2 January: Austrian forces are defeated by the Turks at Kaçanik and are gradually forced to withdraw from Kosovo. In the following months, a Great Serb Migration (*Velika Seoba*) of part of the Serb population of Kosovo and central Serbia takes place northwards to the safety of the Austro-Hungarian Empire.

1737
Early August: Habsburg forces under Field Marshal Friedrich Heinrich von Seckendorf recapture Prishtina, only to abandon Kosovo a few weeks later. More refugees, including some of the Albanian Kelmendi tribe, resettle in Habsburg territory later in 1737 in the so-called Second Migration.

1766
Dissolution of the Greek-dominated Serbian Orthodox Patriarchate of Peja.

1785
Kara Mahmud Pasha Bushatlliu (1749-1796) of Shkodra conquers much of Kosovo.

1822
In an unusual protest march, 3,000 people attempt to walk from Kosovo to Istanbul to demand the removal of the tyrannical Maliq Pasha Gjinolli of Prishtina.

1826
Suppression of the Janissaries throughout the Ottoman Empire.

1830s
A new system of Turkish-language state schools is introduced in Kosovo.

1831
16 July: Bosnian rebel leader Husein of Gradačac defeats Ottoman forces under the Grand Vizier at the Battle of

Lipjan but then, bought by concessions and promises, withdraws to Bosnia.

1836
Opening of two Serb elementary schools in Prizren.

1839
Large uprising in Prizren to protest against Ottoman conscription.

1844
Uprisings in Prishtina and Skopje to protest against the reformed Ottoman conscription and taxation system.

1845
Uprising in Gjakova and western Kosovo.

1855
Uprising in Peja against conscription and taxation.

1860s
Period of relative political stability and harmony in Kosovo.

1866
Uprising in western Kosovo over conscription and taxation. The revolt is heavily suppressed by Ottoman forces in the winter of 1866-1867.

1869
A new Ottoman school law permits teaching in local languages, although not Albanian.

1871
Opening of the Bogoslovija, the Serb Orthodox Seminary in Prizren. **August:** First issue of the journal *Prizren*, with facing pages in Turkish and Serbian. This journal, popular with the Serb community, lasted until 1874.

1874
Opening to the public of the new railway line through Kosovo, from Mitrovica to Skopje and Thessalonika.

1876
2 July: Serbia and Montenegro declare war on Turkey.

1877-1878
The Muslims and Albanians of the sandjak of Niš, some 50,000 individuals, are expelled to Kosovo.

1878
Serb troops occupy parts of Kosovo. **3 March:** Treaty of San Stefano gives Mitrovica and part of the sandjak of Prishtina to Serbia, and the Peja region to Montenegro. **10 June:** Over 300 delegates, mostly Muslims, from throughout Kosovo and Albania gather in Prizren at the so-called Albanian League of Prizren, in response to the Treaty of San Stefano. **13 June-13 July:** Congress of Berlin. **13 June:** The League of Prizren submits an 18-page memorandum to Benjamin Disraeli. **18 June:** Forty-five beys attending the League of Prizren pass and sign the *Kararname*, or resolutions of the gathering, including a demand for Albanian autonomy within the Empire and an end to conscription. **1 September:** Senior Ottoman official Mehmet Ali Pasha arrives in Gjakova as guest of the governor of the town, Abdullah Pasha. The house is

surrounded by angry Albanians, led by Ali Pasha of Gucia and, after a shoot-out, Mehmet Ali and his guards are killed.

1879

October: The members of the League of Prizren agree to accept Abdyl Frashëri's autonomy programme.

1880

Autumn: The League of Prizren is in full control of Kosovo.

1881

March: Ottoman forces are mobilized in Skopje to invade Kosovo. **April:** Prizren is occupied by Ottoman forces and the League of Prizren is dispersed. **May:** Gjakova and Peja are conquered by Ottoman forces.

1884

September: Uprising of the Albanians in the district of Prizren over taxes.

1889

Opening of a Serbian consulate in Prishtina, the first consul, Luka Martinović, being assassinated a year later. **1 May:** The first Albanian-language school opens in Prizren, although still illegal. Among its first teachers are Mati Logoreci and Lazër Lumezi.

1893

Haxhi Zeka and Bajram Curri lead uprisings in Peja, Gjakova and elsewhere in Kosovo, which are quelled by

Ottoman troops. The first Serbian bookshop is opened in Prishtina.

1896
Ottoman decree authorizes the opening of Serb schools in Kosovo, thus indirectly recognizing the Serb nationality.

1897
Haxhi Zeka leads an armed uprising in western Kosovo. In an effort to revive the League of Prizren, he founds the *Besëlidhja shqiptare* (Albanian League).

1899
January: Haxhi Zeka organizes a meeting of 500 leaders in Peja, most of them from Kosovo, that gives rise to the Albanian League of Peja (1899-1900).

1901
Albanian bands pillage and lay waste to Prishtina, Novi Pazar and Sjenica.

1902
31 March: The new Russian consul in Mitrovica, Grigorie Stepanovič Shcherbin, protector of Serb interests, is assassinated by an Albanian.

1903
Austrian statistics for the sandjaks of Prishtina, Peja and Prizren show the proportion of Orthodox Serbs in those regions to be 25 percent. The Mürzsteg Accord of the Great Powers calls upon the sultan to create a new gendarmerie of Christians and Muslims, supervised by

foreign officials. **30 March:** Isa Boletini and 2,000 of his men attack an Ottoman garrison in Mitrovica.

1908
July: Young Turk revolution. **October:** Annexation of Bosnia by Austria-Hungary, and the declaration of complete independence by Bulgaria.

1909
April: Several areas of Kosovo take to arms to protest against the new taxes imposed by the Young Turks. **9 April:** The Sultan Abdul-Hamid II is deposed in Istanbul. **September:** Uprising in the Luma region, southwest of Prizren.

1910
Spring: A tax revolt erupts in northern and northeastern Kosovo and turns into a general uprising throughout the country. **23-29 April:** Idriz Seferi and his 5,000 fighters resist Turkish forces in the gorge of Kaçanik. **June:** The uprising in Kosovo is quelled when Turkish forces take Gjakova and Peja.

1911
15 June: Sultan Mehmet V pays an official visit to Prishtina at the suggestion of the Young Turk government. **16 June:** Sultan Mehmet V, accompanied by the Grand Vizier, visits the tomb of Sultan Murad, north of Prishtina, and proclaims an amnesty for those who participated in the 1910 uprising.

1912

Spring: Beginning of an uprising in many parts of western Kosovo, in particular in Gjakova and Peja. **20 May:** Several thousand Albanian rebels meet in Junik with former parliamentarians Hasan Prishtina and Nexhip Draga, and swear a general *besa* to overthrow the Young Turk regime. **July:** Rebel forces take over Prishtina, Mitrovica, Vushtrria and Ferizaj, and the Turkish governor of Prizren flees to Tetova. **9 August:** The "fourteen point" demands, formulated by Hasan Prishtina, are submitted to the Turkish Government. **14 August:** Sixteen thousand Albanian fighters invade and occupy Skopje. **30 September**: Serbia, Bulgaria and Greece begin a general mobilization of troops. **8 October:** Montenegro declares war on the Ottoman Empire. **16 October:** The Serb Third Army, with 76,000 men, advances into Kosovo. **18 October:** Serbia, Bulgaria and Greece declare war on the Ottoman Empire, thus precipitating the first Balkan War. **22 October:** Serb forces take Prishtina, committing hideous massacres against the Albanian population on their way. **30 October:** Peja falls to the Montenegrin army. **31 October:** Serb forces reach Prizren, which surrenders without a fight on 3 November, and 5,000 Albanians are reportedly slaughtered. **4 November:** Gjakova is attacked by Serb and Montenegrin forces, but is defended staunchly by Bajram Curri and 5,000 Albanian fighters. **28 November:** Ismail Qemal bey Vlora declares Albanian independence in Vlora. **17 December:** Conference of Ambassadors of the Great Powers meets in London to discuss the new situation and territorial changes in the Balkans.

Kosovo under Serb Rule (to 1999)

1913

24 January: In a report to Rome, Lazër Mjeda, Archbishop of Skopje, estimates that 25,000 Albanians were slaughtered by Serb forces during and after the Serb invasion. **22 April:** The citadel of Shkodra, the last Turkish stronghold in the Balkans, is abandoned by Ottoman forces. **30 May:** End of the first Balkan War and peace treaty in London. **July-August:** Second Balkan War. **29 July:** Conference of Ambassadors in London resolves to recognize Albania as a sovereign state, but recognizes Serb claims to Kosovo, Dibra, Ohrid and Monastir. **September:** A large Albanian rebellion in the Luma region and in the mountains west of Gjakova is suppressed by an army of over 20,000 Serb troops who advance into Albania, almost reaching Elbasan. **7 September:** Serbian King Petar I Karadjordjević proclaims the annexation by Serbia of the "conquered territories," including Kosovo.

1914

28 July: Austria-Hungary declares war on Serbia, precipitating World War I, and advances southwards.

1915

21 October: Bulgarian troops invade southeastern Kosovo and take Skopje the following day. **November:** Austro-Hungarian forces reach Kosovo and occupy the northern half of its territory (the southern half being occupied by Bulgaria). **20 November:** The Serb government, whose forces had been routed by Austria-Hungary, decides to evacuate the entire Serb army through the mountains of Albania to the Adriatic coast. **29 November:** Prizren is liberated of Serb forces. A total of 150,000 Serb soldiers are captured during this phase of the campaign. **December:** The Austro-Hungarian authorities install Albanians in local government and allow them to use the Albanian language in the administration. They also encourage the opening of Albanian-language schools.

1916
April: Austro-Hungarian forces demand that Bulgarian troops withdraw from Gjakova, but allow them to keep Prishtina and Prizren.

1918
6 October: German and Austro-Hungarian forces withdraw from Kosovo. **Late October:** The 11th French colonial division takes Prishtina and Mitrovica. The Italian 35th division takes Prizren and pursues the retreating Austro-Hungarian army northwards through Gjakova and Peja. **1 December:** Kosovo, returned to Serb rule, is encompassed within the new Serb-dominated Kingdom of the Serbs, Croats and Slovenes, known from 1929 onward as Yugoslavia.

1919
January-February: According to statistics published in Italy, 6,040 people were killed and 3,873 homes were destroyed by Serb troops in Kosovo. **6 May:** An appeal by the Kosovo Committee for a general uprising leads to a large-scale revolt in Drenica under Azem Galica. **18 December:** Creation in Skopje of the *Islam Muhafaza-yi Hukuk Cemiyeti* (Islamic Association for the Defense of

Justice) Party, known in Albanian as the *Xhemijet*, to represent the interests of Albanian Muslims in Kosovo and Macedonia. Its leader is Nexhip Draga.

1920

September: Yugoslav government "decree on the colonization of the new southern lands" facilitates the takeover by Serb colonists of large Ottoman estates and of land seized from Albanian rebels. Colonist families receive an average of 7.2 hectares of land. Many Albanian families receive land, too, in the framework of an agrarian reform. **November:** Yugoslav army and police units succeed in defeating a large force of Albanian rebels in Drenica. The leaders of the latter, Azem and Shote Galica, flee to Shkodra.

1921

January: A Yugoslav government proclamation calls on Albanian rebels in Kosovo to surrender, offering an amnesty for the period from November 1915 to August 1919. It also authorizes the distribution of arms to the Serb population. **April:** Azem Galica returns to Kosovo to revive resistance.

1928

According to the Serb official, Djordje Krstić, the government colonization programme, which had brought some 70,000 colonists to Kosovo, equivalent to about 10 percent of the total population, raises the proportion of Serbs there from 24 percent in 1919 to 38 percent.

1929

The Kingdom of the Serbs, Croats and Slovenes changes its name to Yugoslavia. **January:** Yugoslavia is divided into nine new administrative units called *banovinas*, Kosovo being partitioned among the *banovinas* of Vardar, Morava and Zeta.

1931

The rail line through Kosovo is extended from Mitrovica to Novi Pazar. **11 June:** New Yugoslav law "on the colonization of the southern regions" enters into force.

1933

The Yugoslav government begins negotiations with the Turkish government for the deportation of the Muslim Albanian population to Turkey. **14 August:** Hasan Prishtina is assassinated by an agent of King Zog at the Café Astoria in Thessalonika.

1934

A new rail line connects Fushë Kosova and Prishtina.

1935

Beginning of an orchestrated wave of confiscation of land from Albanians in Kosovo. **August:** The first cell of the Yugoslav communist party is formed in Mitrovica.

1936

A new rail line connects Fushë Kosova and Peja.

1937

7 March: Vaso Čubrilović presents his memorandum on the expulsion of the Albanians from Kosovo. **July:**

Foundation in Peja of the provincial committee for Kosovo of the Yugoslav communist party.

1941

6 April: German troops invade Yugoslavia and Greece. All of Kosovo is occupied by Italian, German and Bulgarian forces within one week. **17 April:** Yugoslavia surrenders unconditionally to Axis forces. **21 April:** The Italian and German foreign ministers, meeting in Vienna, agree that most of the Albanian-inhabited parts of Kosovo should be put under Italian control and be united with Albania. **21 April:** German division commander, General Eberhardt, meets in Mitrovica with Albanian leaders, among whom is Xhafer Deva, to formalize the Albanian takeover of local government and to discuss the expulsion of Serb and Montenegrin colonists from Kosovo. **May:** Montenegrin colonists settled in and around Peja are driven out of Kosovo by local Albanians. In the following two to three months, an estimated 20,000 colonists flee. **29 June:** Benito Mussolini proclaims Greater Albania. **July:** Most of Kosovo, under Italian occupation, is united with Albania.

1943

8 September: Italy capitulates to Allied forces. **Mid-September:** a large public meeting is held by Albanian leaders in Prizren, under German occupation, to proclaim a second League of Prizren in order to defend Kosovo from Yugoslav encroachments. During the following months, it is also involved in the expulsion of Serb and Montenegrin colonists.

1943-1944

31 December 1943 to 2 January 1944: Conference of Bujan takes place, during which the Kosovo provincial committee of the communist party of Yugoslavia demands the right to self-determination and to reunite Kosovo with Albania after the war.

1944

May: The Skanderbeg SS Division rounds up 281 Jews who are deported and sent to their deaths in Bergen-Belsen. **September:** German troops withdraw from Greece and retreat northwards through Kosovo. **19 November**: German troops abandon Prishtina and withdraw from Kosovo.

1945

8 February: Introduction of Yugoslav military rule in Kosovo. **16 March:** Tito issues a provisional decree banning the return of Serb colonists to Kosovo, but changes his mind two weeks later. **29 April:** Yugoslavia becomes the first country to recognize the new communist regime in Albania. **3 September:** The presidency of the People's Assembly of Serbia passes a law on the establishment of the "Autonomous Region of Kosovo and Metohija" as a constituent part of Serbia.

1946

9 July: Treaty on friendship, cooperation and mutual assistance between Yugoslavia and Albania. **27 November:** Treaty on a customs union between Yugoslavia and Albania.

1947

A new rail line connects Prishtina with Podujeva, extending to Niš in southern Serbia.

1948

28 June: Yugoslavia is expelled from the Cominform after a Warsaw conference of communist parties. **30 June:** Albania renounces all economic agreements with Yugoslavia. The border between the two countries is hermetically sealed.

1949

12 November: Yugoslavia renounces the pact of friendship, cooperation and mutual assistance with Albania.

1950

11 October: Yugoslavia breaks off diplomatic ties with Albania.

1953

Yugoslavia signs agreements with Turkey and Greece, facilitating the large-scale emigration of Yugoslav "Turks," who in reality are mostly Muslim Kosovo Albanians, to Turkey. An initial wave of 13,000 "Turks" leaves Kosovo for Turkey. **22 December:** Resumption of formal diplomatic relations between Yugoslavia and Albania.

1956

Repressive campaign by the Yugoslav secret police to collect weapons from the Kosovo Albanian population. Thousands of families flee to Turkey. **June-July:** The so-called Prizren Trial, in which the Department of State Security (UDBA) claimed to have uncovered a network of spies and agents from Albania, results in long prison sentences for the nine accused. Twelve years later, all of the prisoners are released and declared innocent.

1963
Under the new Yugoslav constitution, Kosovo receives limited autonomy within Serbia and is officially known as the "Autonomous Province of Kosovo and Metohija." Its constitutional status at the federal level is virtually eliminated. A new rail line connects Peja and Prizren.

1966
1 July: The purging of Aleksandar Ranković, Serb strongman and minister of the interior, at the Brioni Plenum marks the beginning of an improvement in the situation of the Kosovo Albanians.

1967
March: Tito pays his first visit to Kosovo in 16 years.

1968
Official usage of the pejorative BCS term for the Albanians, *šiptar*, is banned in favor of the neutral term *albanac*. **October-November:** Demonstrations and unrest for republic status are forcefully quelled by the Yugoslav police and army. The slogan "Kosovo-Republic!" is heard in public for the first time on 27 November. **16-18 December:** An amendment to the Yugoslav Constitution makes Kosovo a constituent element of the Yugoslav federation. The old official designation "Kosovo and Metohija," or "Kosmet," is replaced by the simple

word "Kosovo," more to the liking of the Albanian population.

1969
The Kosovo Albanians win the right to fly their own national flag. **April:** Yugoslavia and Albania sign an agreement on road transport.

1970
15 February: Foundation of the University of Prishtina.

1971
February: The establishment of diplomatic relations between Albania and Yugoslavia brings about a thaw in cultural relations with Kosovo.

1972
Orthography Congress in Tirana at which delegates from Albania, Kosovo and elsewhere agree upon a definitive orthography for the Albanian language.

1974
21, 25, 28 February: New constitutions are promulgated for Yugoslavia, Serbia and Kosovo, giving the province a status virtually equal to that of a Yugoslav republic.

1981
March-April: Student demonstrations for further autonomy are denounced by the communist party leadership as counterrevolutionary. Dozens of people are killed and thousands are imprisoned. Belgrade imposes a state of siege. **July-August:** Purge, or "differentiation," in the communist party leadership in Kosovo.

1982

17 January: Political activists Jusuf and Bardhosh Gërvalla and Kadri Zeka are assassinated in Stuttgart.

1986

Memorandum by leading members of the Serbian Academy of Sciences and Arts (SANU) describes the situation in Kosovo as "genocide" and calls for a restoration of direct Serb rule.

1987

24 April: Slobodan Milošević goes to Kosovo to listen to the grievances of Kosovo Serbs and declares before them: "Let no one ever dare to beat the (Serb) people!"

1988

Mass demonstrations by the Kosovo Albanians against the policies of Slobodan Milošević. **17 November:** Milošević dismisses the Albanian communist leaders of Kosovo. In reaction, the Trepça miners emerge from their pit and march on Prishtina. **18 November:** Factory workers, students and children join the march of an estimated 100,000 people.

1989

18-28 February: Hunger strike of 1,300 miners in Trepça. **3 March:** Arrest of Azem Vllasi. **28 March:** The Serb Parliament suspends and de facto eliminates the autonomy of Kosovo. Albanian protests are put down by force. **April:** Mass arrests of Albanians; over 1,000 workers are put on trial in Ferizaj alone. **June:** One million Serbs gather at Gazimestan, north of Prishtina, to commemorate the 600th anniversary of the Battle of Kosovo Polje. Serb nationalism, whipped up by Milošević, reaches a peak. **30 October:** Opening of the trial of Azem Vllasi. **23 December:** Official founding of the Democratic League of Kosovo (LDK).

1990

22 March: The Serb parliament invokes a "programme for the attainment of peace, freedom and prosperity in the Socialist Autonomous Province of Kosovo" to provide financial support to Kosovo Serbs and to encourage Kosovo Albanians to emigrate. **28 April:** Adem Demaçi is released from prison after 28 years of incarceration. **April-May:** Thousands of Albanian school children are taken to hospital suffering from stomach pains, headaches and nausea. The Albanian population suspects a mass poisoning, whereas the Serb authorities speak of mass hysteria. **May:** An amendment to the Serb law on universities makes the use of "minority languages" illegal at universities in Kosovo. **26 June:** Using "temporary measures," the Serb government and administrative authorities take over provincial competencies by virtue of a new law on the "Activities of the Institutions of the Republic under Exceptional Circumstances." **2 July:** Kosovo Albanian declaration of independence. One hundred fourteen of the 123 members of the parliament of Kosovo, meeting in the street outside their locked assembly building, declare Kosovo to be an "equal and independent entity within the framework of the Yugoslav federation," i.e., a Yugoslav "Republic of Kosovo." **5 July:** Serb forces break up the parliament and government of Kosovo, and shut down Albanian-language media. RTV Prishtina and Albanian-language newspapers cease functioning. **7 July:** The Belgrade authorities permanently abolish the parliament and government institutions of Kosovo. Beginning of open apartheid in Kosovo. **7 September:** Kosovo parliamentarians, gathering secretly in Kaçanik, promulgate a new constitution for the Republic of Kosovo. Kosovo is to be a sovereign state among the other nations of Yugoslavia. The Belgrade authorities transform Kosovo into a Serb protectorate run by a Serb governor. **December:** Serb soldiers are posted in front of secondary schools in Kosovo to assure that no Albanian pupils or teachers enter, unless they agree to the newly imposed Serb curricula.

1991
20-21 May: Weapons are distributed to Kosovo Serb civilians in Kosovo. **22 September:** Declaration of the independence of the "Republic of Kosovo" by the "underground" parliament of Kosovo. **26-30 September:** A referendum on independence is held among the population of Kosovo. 99.86 percent of those who take part in the referendum (participation 87.01 percent) vote for independence. **19 October:** Parliament declares the independent "Republic of Kosovo," and selects Bujar Bukoshi as prime minister of a new government in exile.

1992
7 May: *Rilindja* newspaper begins publication in exile in Switzerland. **24 May:** parliamentary and presidential elections are held in Kosovo during which the LDK receives 76.4 percent of votes and Ibrahim Rugova is elected as president of the republic by 99.5 percent of ballots cast.

1993
28 July: The Belgrade government expels the members of the Observer Mission for Kosovo, the Sandjak and the Vojvodina of the Organization for Security and Cooperation in Europe (OCSE), which had been in place since September 1992.

1994
23 February: The Serb authorities close down the Academy of Sciences and Arts of Kosovo.

1995
21 November: The Dayton Agreement, designed to bring peace to the Balkans, makes only a brief reference to Kosovo in an appendix.

1996
29 January: Decision by the European Union Council of Ministers to make the international recognition of the Federal Republic of Yugoslavia dependent upon the human rights situation in Kosovo. **April:** Beginning of coordinated attacks by the Kosovo Liberation Army on persons representing and collaborating with the Serb regime. **5 June:** U.S. Deputy Secretary of State John Kornblum opens a United States Information Center in Prishtina. **1 September:** With mediation from the Catholic Communità di Sant' Egidio, Slobodan Milošević and Ibrahim Rugova separately sign an agreement on the "Normalization of the Albanian Education System at all Levels," but the agreement is never implemented. **December:** Students at the University of Prishtina criticize not only Milošević, but also Rugova for the lack of implementation of the education agreement.

1997

16 January: The Serb rector of the University of Prishtina, Radivoje Papović, and his driver, are wounded in an assassination attempt. **8 August:** Kosovo Liberation Army (KLA) publicly assumes responsibility for armed attacks against "Serb occupants and Albanian collaborators" in Kosovo. **28 October:** The KLA makes its first public appearance at a funeral in Drenica. **29 October:** Twenty thousand students demonstrate peacefully for the return of school and university property; 200 demonstrators are injured by Serb forces. **21 November:** Six political parties and associations join to create a Democratic Forum of Albanian intellectuals, as an alternative to Ibrahim Rugova's Democratic League of Kosovo. Chairperson of the new forum is Rexhep Qosja. **25-28 November:** Fighting around Skenderaj in Kosovo causes several deaths. **30 December:** Tens of thousands of people demonstrate in Prishtina against the ban on education.

1998

24 January: Local Serb politician, Desimir Vasić, is shot and killed in an attack in Skenderaj. **1 March:** Serb troops begin a major offensive in the Drenica region of Kosovo, attacking the villages of Çirez and Likoshana. Twenty to 30 people die in the fighting. Serb hospitals refuse to treat injured Albanians. **4 March:** The KLA issues a communiqué calling on all Albanians to join the fight against the Serbs. **7 March:** Warlord Adem Jashari is slain after a three-day shootout with Serb forces that surrounded his home in Prekaz in the Drenica region. **9 March:** Over 200,000 Kosovo Albanians demonstrate in Prishtina and are beaten back by the Serb police. **15 May:** U.S. intermediary Richard Holbrooke arranges a meeting in Belgrade between Slobodan Milošević and a 15-member Kosovar delegation under Ibrahim Rugova. **18 May:** Hundreds of Serb students devastate the premises of the Albanological Institute and the Faculty of Technology in Prishtina to protest against the return of parts of the university to the Albanians. **29 May:** The Council for the Defense of Human Rights and Freedoms in Prishtina reports that one-fourth of the territory of Kosovo, inhabited by 700,000 people, is now a war zone. **June:** Thousands of Kosovo Albanian refugees flee to Albania. The North Atlantic Treaty Organization (NATO) begins to overfly Kosovo. **29 June:** Serb offensive near Prishtina and Kijeva. **3 July:** Kijeva falls to Serb forces after several weeks under KLA control. **16 July:** An attempt is made to reassemble the parliament of Kosovo. **28 July:** Serb forces recapture Malisheva. **30 July:** Serb forces recapture Rahovec, killing sixty Albanians and wounding 227. **4 August:** Massacre of Kosovo Albanian civilians in Rahovec. Llausha in the Drenica region is captured by Serb forces and is razed to the ground. **13 August:** The KLA appoints seven political representatives to negotiate with Belgrade. Among them are Jakup Krasniqi and Adem Demaçi. **16 August:** Serb forces recapture Junik after weeks of fighting. **29 August:** Belgrade accuses the KLA of the massacre of 22 Serb civilians in Kleçka. **21 September:** Ahmet Krasniqi, minister of defence of the Kosovar government in exile, is assassinated in Tirana. **23 September:** UN Security Council Resolution 1199 condemns the unjustified use of force by Serb security forces in Kosovo. **24 September:** The NATO Council activates orders to prepare for military action in Kosovo.

28 September: International observers report on the massacre of Albanian civilians in Abria e Epërme, Vraniq and Gollobovc. **8 October:** The KLA agrees to a cease-fire to come into effect on 9 October. **13 October:** Slobodan Milošević agrees to withdraw his forces from Kosovo and to allow the deployment of a Kosovo Verification Mission under U.S. diplomat William Walker. An estimated 330,000 Kosovo Albanians have been put to flight. **17 October:** Renewed clashes between the KLA and the Serb army. **22 October:** Ibrahim Rugova is awarded the annual Sakharov Prize by the European Parliament. **14 December:** At least 36 Kosovo Albanian fighters are shot to death by Serb troops at the Albania-Kosovo border. **18 December:** The corpse of the kidnaped deputy mayor of Fushë Kosova (Kosovo Polje), Zvonko Bojanić, is discovered. **24-27 December:** Serb offensive in Podujeva, following the death of a Serb policeman there. The KLA offers a cease-fire.

1999
5 January: The head of the Serb resistance movement in Kosovo, Momčilo Trajković, announces the formation of a Serb National Council to protect Serb interests in Kosovo, if the Belgrade government refuses to do so. **11 January:** The head of the Kosovo Information Center (QIK), Enver Maloku, is murdered in Prishtina. **15 January:** The massacre by the Serb police of 45 Kosovo Albanian civilians in Reçak (BCS Račak) causes international outrage after an OCSE delegation under William Walker discovers the bodies. **24 January:** Serb forces and the KLA exchange prisoners. **25 January:** Five Albanian civilians, including two children, are shot by Serb forces in Rakovina. **29 January:** The bodies of

twenty-four Albanians are found in Rogova. **30 January:** The secretary-general of NATO authorizes air strikes against Yugoslavia. **3 February:** The KLA declares its willingness to send a delegation to peace negotiations in France. **6-23 February:** The Rambouillet Conference, organized by the French and British foreign ministers, Hubert Védrine and Robin Cook, is held to avoid full-scale war in Kosovo. **23 February:** The three main Albanian political formations, the Democratic League of Kosovo (LDK) under Ibrahim Rugova, the United Democratic Movement (LBD) under Rexhep Qosja and the Kosovo Liberation Army under Hashim Thaçi, sign an agreement in Rambouillet to form a provisional government to represent Kosovo Albanians until free elections can be held. **2 March:** The KLA nominates Hashim Thaçi, head of its political directorate, to serve as prime minister of the provisional government of Kosovo. Adem Demaçi resigns as the political representative of the KLA. **13 March:** The Albanian-language daily newspapers *Kosovo Sot* (Kosovo Today) and *Gazeta Shqiptare* (The Albanian Gazette) are fined about DM 100,000 each for "supporting terrorism." **15-19 March:** Further negotiations in Paris. **18 March:** The Albanian delegation to the Paris peace talks signs the peace agreement. The Serb delegation refuses to sign. **19-20 March:** The OSCE mission withdraws definitively from Kosovo. **20 March:** Massive escalation of the Serb offensive against Kosovo Albanian villages and towns, following the OSCE withdrawal. **24 March:** Beginning of the NATO bombing campaign. **25 March:** Russia protests against the NATO bombing campaign and expresses its support for Serbia. Yugoslavia breaks off diplomatic relations with the United States, Germany, France and the United Kingdom. **26 March-April:** Serb forces begin

56

with the implementation of Operation Horseshoe to cleanse Kosovo of its majority Albanian population. **27 March:** Museum of the League of Prizren is destroyed. **30 March:** The old town of Gjakova is set on fire and razed to the ground. **1 April:** Serb television broadcasts footage of a meeting in Belgrade between Slobodan Milošević and Ibrahim Rugova. **2 April:** The KLA forms a provisional government for Kosovo under Hashim Thaçi. **14 April:** NATO aircraft mistakenly bomb a convoy of Albanian refugees, killing 60 people. **30 April:** The Albanian population in the southern Serbian regions of Presheva, Bujanoc and Medvegja is put to flight. **5 May:** Ibrahim Rugova arrives in Rome. **7 May:** Fehmi Agani is murdered by Serb paramilitaries while being expelled to Macedonia by train. **14 May:** NATO aircraft bomb the village of Korisha near Prizren, mistakenly killing about 100 civilians. **22 May:** President Slobodan Milošević, President Milan Milutinović, Deputy Prime Minister Nikola Šainović, Minister of the Interior Vlajko Stojiljković and army chief-of-staff Dragoljub Ojdanić are indicted by The Hague Tribunal for crimes against humanity and violations of the laws or customs of war in Kosovo. **3 June:** The Serb parliament votes to accept the demands of the G8 countries and to withdraw its forces from Kosovo. **9 June:** A Military Technical Agreement is signed in Kumanovo, Macedonia, between the Kosovo Force (KFOR) and the Government of Yugoslavia, specifying the withdrawal of Serb forces from Kosovo within 11 days. NATO forces enter Kosovo. **10 June:** The United Nations Security Council adopts Resolution 1244 on Kosovo. NATO Secretary-General Javier Solana orders an interruption of the bombing campaign. **13 June:** During their withdrawal from Prishtina, Serb troops set fire to the historical archives of the Islamic community. **18 June:** KFOR troops free a group of 10 to 15 Serbs and Roma held prisoner and mishandled by the KLA. The head of the new provisional government, Hashim Thaçi, calls on the Kosovo Serb population to remain in the country. **20 June:** Serb forces complete their withdrawal from Kosovo, and NATO formally suspends the bombing campaign.

Kosovo under United Nations Administration (1999-2008)

1999

29 June: Thirteen Albanian parties and political groups meet in Prishtina to discuss the formation of a broader government. **1 July:** The OSCE sets up a mission in Kosovo, to be known as the United Nations Interim Administration Mission in Kosovo (UNMIK). **2 July:** Bernard Kouchner is appointed Special Representative of the UN Secretary-General, thus becoming head of the UNMIK administration. **5 July:** Foundation in Prishtina of the Democratic Union Party (Partia e Bashkimit Demokratik), headed by KLA commander Bardhyl Mahmuti. **16 July:** First meeting of the Kosovo Transitional Council as an initial step towards self-government. **23 July:** Fourteen Serb farmers are murdered by Albanian extremists in Gracka, near Lipjan. **30 July:** A new Serb national assembly is formed in Zveçan to defend the rights of the Kosovo Serb minority. **2 August:** The University of Prishtina is reopened by rector Zenel Kelmendi, after eight years of Serb occupation. **3 August:** Nearly 90 percent of the more than 850,000 Kosovar refugees abroad have returned to Kosovo. **18 August:** Agim Çeku, chief of staff of the KLA, denounces acts of violence committed against non-Albanians and calls on the latter to remain in Kosovo. **21 August:** Opening of a police academy in Prishtina, in which 200 young policemen and policewomen are to be trained. **31 August:** According to the UNHCR, about 300,000 people in Kosovo are without shelter. **5 September:** Ethnic unrest in Mitrovica and in the area of the Trepça mines. **6 September:** The Deutschmark is declared to be the official currency of Kosovo, replacing the Yugoslav dinar. **19 September:** Radio and Television of Kosovo (RTK) begins broadcasting. **20 September:** KFOR and the KLA agree to the transformation of the latter into the Kosovo Protection Corps, subordinate to the UN Special Representative. **1 October:** The United Nations "Blue Sky" public radio begins broadcasting, with a twenty-four-hour mix of UNMIK news, music and features. **13 October:** Hashim Thaçi, head of the provisional government, and Bardhyl Mahmuti, head of the Democratic Union Party, agree to found the Democratic Progress Party, with Thaçi as its chairperson, Mahmuti as deputy chairperson and Jakup Krasniqi as general secretary. **13-14 October:** UN Secretary-General Kofi Annan visits Kosovo. **18 October:** At a meeting in Graçanica under Orthodox Bishop Artemije Radosavljević, the Kosovo Serb community founds a 49-member Serb National Council. **9 December:** Writer and human rights activist Flora Brovina is sentenced by a Belgrade court to 12 years in prison for "terrorism." **10 December:** In Prishtina about 200,000 people protest to demand the release of Albanian prisoners in Serb jails and prisons. **15 December:** UNMIK and the three major political parties in Kosovo agree to the setting up of a Joint Interim Administrative Structure (JIAS) and an eight-member Interim Administrative Council to replace the provisional government of Hashim Thaçi and the presidential rule of Ibrahim Rugova. Serb representatives refuse to participate in the council.

2000

11 January: The Interim Administrative Council begins functioning, with the allocation of the proposed administrative departments to the political parties. Prishtina's Sllatina airport reopens for civilian aircraft. **31 January:** Tension in the Presheva valley in southern Serbia. **1 February:** Ibrahim Rugova announces that the organs of the Republic of Kosovo are henceforth dissolved. **3 February:** Outbreak of violence in Mitrovica, leaving eight Albanians dead, after the attack on a UN bus the day before, in which two elderly Serbs were killed. **9 February:** First meeting of the expanded, 34-member Kosovo Transitional Council, now including representatives of civil society, religious communities and minorities. **25-26 February:** A blaze destroys the Boro and Ramiz Sports Center in Prishtina. **March:** Violence in the Presheva valley causes a wave of some 5,000 refugees to flee to Kosovo and Macedonia. **13 March:** Kosovo student leader Albin Kurti is sentenced by a Serb court in Niš to 15 years in prison for "activities against the territorial integrity of Yugoslavia." **14 March:** Kosovo issues its first postage stamps. **15 March:** Unrest in Mitrovica. **2 April:** The Serb National Council agrees to participate in the Interim Administrative Council as observers. **18 April:** A mass trial begins in Niš of 145 Albanians accused of attacks on the Serb army and police in Gjakova in the spring of 1999. **8 May:** Assassination in Prizren of the moderate KLA commander, Ekrem Rexha, known as Commander Drini. **21-22 May:** First party congress of the PPDK in Prishtina, which votes to change its name to Democratic Party of Kosovo (PDK). **22 May:** Despite international and UNMIK protests, a Serb court of law in Niš sentences 143 Kosovo Albanian prisoners to a total of 1,632 years in prison for so-called "terrorist activities." **31 May:** International postal services begin to function. **15 June:** Four hundred KFOR troops begin a campaign to collect weapons in the Drenica Valley. Tons of arms are discovered and confiscated. **7 July:** Politician Ramush Haradinaj and his brother Daut are severely wounded in an explosion in Strellc. The leader of the Alliance for the Future of Kosovo (AAK) is flown to Germany for treatment and returns to Kosovo on 18 July. **10 July:** New electoral law for Kosovo is signed into force by Special Representative Kouchner. **15 July:** A series of ethnically motivated armed attacks involving Serb and Albanian extremists takes place in Mitrovica. **24 July:** U.S. President George W. Bush visits Kosovo and endorses UNMIK efforts to prepare the Kosovars for taking on greater responsibility in "running their own affairs." **August:** Numerous violent attacks against the Serb minority. **28 October:** The first free local elections are held in Kosovo. Ibrahim Rugova's LDK wins 58 percent of the popular vote, Hashim Thaçi's PDK wins 27.3 percent and Ramush Haradinaj's AAK 7.7 percent. **1 November:** Flora Brovina is released from prison in Serbia. **22 November:** A bomb attack is carried out in Prishtina against the building housing the office of the representative of the Yugoslav Government, Stanimir Vikučević. Four persons are injured in the blast.

December: Renewed fighting in the Presheva valley. **16 December:** Rexhep Qosja resigns as head of the United Democratic Movement (LBD).

2001

January: Ethnic tension in Macedonia turns into an armed conflict between the Albanian-backed National Liberation Army and the Macedonian armed forces. **15 January:** Former Danish defense minister Hans Haekkerup takes office as UN Special Representative in Kosovo, replacing Bernard Kouchner. **17 January:** Albania and Yugoslavia resume diplomatic relations. **27 January:** First UNMIK travel documents are distributed, thus enabling Kosovo Albanians to apply for visas and to travel abroad to the 16 countries recognizing the new documents. **29 January:** Unrest in Mitrovica when Serb extremists attack the so-called Bosnian quarter of the town, inhabited by Albanians and Bosniacs. **16 February:** A terrorist attack on a convoy of buses carrying Kosovo Serb civilians leaves 10 people killed and dozens injured. **11 March:** NATO mediators arrange a cease-fire between the Belgrade authorities and the Liberation Army for Presheva, Medvegja and Bujanoc (UÇPMB) in southern Serbia. **14 March:** Heavy fighting in and around Tetova in western Macedonia. **23 March:** In a joint declaration, the leaders of the three major political parties in Kosovo, Ibrahim Rugova, Hashim Thaçi and Ramush Haradinaj, call upon "extremist groups who have taken to arms in the territory of Macedonia to put down their weapons," and appeal to the Macedonian Government to use peaceful means to solve the crisis. **25-26 March:** Large sections of the Albanian population in parts of Macedonia flee to Kosovo in the wake of a new offensive by Macedonian troops. **18 April:** The head of the Yugoslav passport office and five other Serbs are killed in a bomb attack in Prishtina. The attack is later attributed to the German KLA mercenary, Roland Bartetzko. **15 May:** Serious fighting flares up in the Presheva valley between Yugoslav forces and the UÇPMB. Promulgation of the Constitutional Framework for Provisional Self-Government. **3 June:** Discovery of a mass grave near Belgrade containing the bodies of 86 Kosovo Albanian civilians and fighters murdered in the spring of 1999. **12 June:** Thousands of ethnic Albanians continue to flee into Kosovo from the fighting in Macedonia. **13 August:** The central electoral commission admits 10 political parties for participation in the coming elections in Kosovo: the Democratic League of Kosovo (LDK), the Democratic Party of Kosovo (PDK), the Alliance for the Future of Kosovo (AAK), the Albanian Christian Democratic Party of Kosovo (PSHDK), the Ashkali Albanian Democratic Party of Kosovo (PDASHK), the Liberal Party of Kosovo (PLK), the Social Democratic Party of Kosovo (PSDK), the Liberal Center Party of Kosovo (PQLK), the Albanian National Democratic Party of Kosovo (PNDSHK), and the Green Party of Kosovo (PGJK). **6 September:** The OSCE requires at least one-third of the candidates of each political party taking part in the parliamentary elections in Kosovo to be women. **2 October:** The interim council that united representatives of most of the political and ethnic groups in Kosovo two years earlier is dissolved in preparation for coming parliamentary elections. **17 November:** Parliamentary elections are held in Kosovo, organized by the OSCE. The LDK of Ibrahim Rugova wins 46.3 percent of the vote, the PDK of Hashim Thaçi 25.5 percent, the Serb coalition Povratak 11 percent and the AAK of Ramush Haradinaj 7.8 percent. The seats in parliament are thus divided as follows: LDK 47, PDK 26, Povratak 22, AAK 8, the Bosnian parties 5, the Turkish Democratic Party 2, the Ashkali Albanian Democratic Party 2, and others 8. **28 November:** A monumental equestrian statue of Scanderbeg, created by Albanian sculptor Janaq Paço, is set up on the main street of Prishtina to commemorate the Albanian national holiday. **7 December:** Kosovo student leader Albin Kurti is released from prison in Serbia. **10 December:** The first session of the new Kosovo parliament is opened by UN Special Representative Hans Haekkerup. LDK member Nexhat Daci is elected as speaker of the house, despite the vociferous protest of PDK leader Hashim Thaçi. **13 December:** Ibrahim Rugova receives only 49 of the 80 votes in parliament that he needs to become President of Kosovo.

2002
1 January: Introduction of the Euro as the official currency of Kosovo. **10 January:** Rugova receives insufficient support in the second and third round of voting for the office of president of Kosovo. **23 January:** Michael Steiner, advisor to German Chancellor Gerhard Schröder, is appointed to replace Hans Haekkerup as UN Special Representative in Kosovo. Steiner assumes office on 14 February. **12 February:** Beginning of the Milošević trial in The Hague. **28 February:** The three main Albanian political parties finally agree upon a coalition government, three and a half months after the parliamentary elections. Bajram Rexhepi is nominated by the Democratic Party as prime minister, and the three parties agree to elect Ibrahim Rugova as president. **4 March:** In an 88 to three vote in

parliament, Ibrahim Rugova is elected president of Kosovo and Bajram Rexhepi is made prime minister. **April:** Special Representative Michael Steiner sets forth the eight benchmarks of his "Standards before Status" approach to Kosovo's future. **19 June:** The UN police arrest several KPC officers on accusations of crimes committed against Albanians in 1999. Among the arrested are Daut Haradinaj, brother of AAK party leader Ramush Haradinaj. **29 June:** The second party conference of the Democratic Party of Kosovo confirms Hashim Thaçi as party head. He declares the fight against crime and corruption to be his primary political goal. **11 August:** Former KLA commander Rrustem Mustafa, known as Remi, is arrested by the UN police on charges of torturing and murdering prisoners. **12 August:** AAK party leader Ramush Haradinaj is indicted, though not arrested, for a shooting incident in 2000. **13 August:** An agreement on cultural cooperation is signed between Kosovo and Albania. **2 September:** UN Special Representative Michael Steiner opens a multi-ethnic cultural center in Mitrovica. Albanian Prime Minister Fatos Nano meets Yugoslav President Vojislav Koštunica in Johannesburg and the two countries agree to exchange ambassadors. **20 September:** Trade agreement between Yugoslavia and Albania. **29 September:** Kosovo Serbs, casting their ballots in the Serbian presidential elections, vote 60 percent for Vojislav Šešelj, candidate of the right-wing extremist Serbian Radical Party. The vast majority of Albanian voters in southern Serbia boycott the elections. **21 October:** Steiner presents a decentralization plan for Kosovo, giving ethnic minorities the opportunity to create administrative units of their own. **26 October:** Local elections are held in Kosovo for the second time. With

55 percent of the ca. 1.3 million eligible voters and only 20 percent of eligible Serb voters taking part. The results give the LDK the absolute majority in 11 of the 30 municipalities and a relative majority in eight municipalities. The Democratic Party receives an absolute majority in four municipalities. The Serb parties win five municipalities. **12 November:** The cabinet of Prime Minister Bajram Rexhepi is finally sworn in. **25 November:** After reaching an agreement with Belgrade, the UNMIK authorities dissolve the parallel Serb administrative structures running northern Mitrovica and place the town under UNMIK administration. **12 December:** The railway link between Kosovo and Serbia is restored for the first time since the war.

2003
20 January: Former Serb president, Milan Milutinović, is extradited from Belgrade to The Hague to face charges for war crimes in Kosovo. **18 February:** Fatmir Limaj, member of parliament for the Democratic Party, is arrested in Slovenia on a mandate of the International Criminal Tribunal for Former Yugoslavia (ICTY) and extradited to The Hague. **12 March:** The prime minister of Serbia, Zoran Djindjić, is assassinated in Belgrade. He is succeeded in office on 18 March by Zoran Živković. **9 April:** Russia withdraws its troops from the KFOR mission and thus from Kosovo. **28 May:** UNMIK transfers 19 of the 44 competences defined in the constitutional framework to the Government of Kosovo, including agriculture and justice. **4 June:** Three members of the Serb Stolić family from Obiliq are murdered by persons unknown, causing much unrest in the Kosovo Serb community. **7 July:** In a public gesture of reconciliation,

President Rugova and the heads of the three main Albanian political parties call upon Kosovo Serb refugees who fled Kosovo during or after the war to return home. A "technical" free trade agreement between Kosovo and Albania is signed by Michael Steiner and the Albanian minister of economics, Arben Malaj. **11 July:** Kosovo ombudsman, Marek Novicki, publishes an annual report accusing the UNMIK authorities of repeated violations of human and civil rights in Kosovo. **26 July:** The former Finnish prime minister, Harri Holkeri, is appointed as the new head of UNMIK, succeeding Michael Steiner. Holkeri assumes office on 26 August. **8 November:** The People's Movement of Kosovo (LPK) presents a petition signed by 46,000 people to the parliament of Kosovo for reunification with Albania. **10 December:** The "Standards for Kosovo," inspired by Steiner's eight-point "Standards before Status," are set forth and presented in Prishtina.

2004

17-18 March: Major outbreak of ethnic violence throughout Kosovo, resulting in 19 deaths, of whom there are 11 Albanians and eight Serbs, and about 900 injuries. About 700, mostly Serb and Roma, homes and 30 churches and cultural sites are damaged or destroyed. At least 3,000 Serbs are driven from their homes in what proves to be a major setback to the process of conciliation. **16 June:** UN Secretary-General Kofi Annan appoints the Danish diplomat, Søren Jessen-Petersen, as his new Special Representative in Kosovo. **17 June:** United Nations police arrest about 270 people in connection with the rioting in mid-March. **23 October:** Parliamentary elections are held in Kosovo. The LDK wins 45.4 percent of the vote, the PDK 28.9 percent, the ΛΛK 8.4 percent and the Ora initiative of Veton Surroi 6.2 percent. The seats in parliament are thus divided as follows: LDK 47, PDK 30, AAK 9, Ora 7, Christian-Democratic Party 2, and five other parties with one seat each. The Serb parties boycott the elections, but receive a guaranteed 10 seats. The non-Serb minorities also receive 10 seats. **15 November:** Start of first trial of Kosovo Albanians at The Hague Tribunal: Fatmir Limaj, Haradin Balaj and Isak Musliu. **17 November:** The LDK and AAK parties agree on a new government coalition. Ramush Haradinaj becomes prime minister.

2005

8 March: Ramush Haradinaj resigns as prime minister after being indicted for war crimes by The Hague Tribunal, and surrenders voluntarily to The Hague the next day. He is replaced in office by Bajram Kosumi, also of the AAK. **3 May:** Kosovo signs credit agreement with the European Investment Bank, allowing for international loans without Serb interference. **4 June:** Kosovo Serbs announce end of their boycott of Kosovar government institutions. **5 September:** President Rugova is diagnosed with lung cancer.

2006

21 January: Death of Ibrahim Rugova. **10 February:** Fatmir Sejdiu is elected president of Kosovo. **20 February:** Beginning of negotiations in Vienna between Kosovo and Serbia on the country's status. **1 March:** Prime Minister Bajram Kosumi resigns as prime minister. Nexhat Daci of the LDK loses his position as speaker of parliament. **10 March:** Kolë Berisha is elected as speaker of parliament. Agim Çeku of the AAK is elected by parliament as prime minister. **11 March:** Death of Serbian dictator Slobodan Milošević in detention in The Hague. **24 July:** President Sejdiu and Prime Minister Çeku meet with Serb President Tadić and Serb Prime Minister Koštunica in Vienna in the presence of negotiator Martti Ahtissaari. **1 September:** German diplomat Joachim Rücker appointed Special Representative of the UNMIK administration, replacing Søren Jessen-Petersen. **28-29 October:** A national referendum in Serbia approves by 51.5 percent a new Serb Constitution that claims Kosovo as an "integral part of Serbia with substantial autonomy." **9 December:** Kosovar President Fatmir Sejdiu is elected as head of the LDK over his rival Nexhat Daci.

2007

12 January: The LDK splits into two factions, with the new faction under Nexhat Daci calling itself the Democratic League of Dardania. **26 January**: UN Special Envoy Martti Ahtisaari presents his settlement proposal for Kosovo independence, as the basis for a UN Security Council resolution. **10 February**: Two people are killed in protests in Prishtina by the *Vetëvendosje M*ovement against the Ahtisaari Plan. **26 March:** The European Union, NATO and the United States express their support for the Ahtisaari Plan for internationally supervised independence. **10 June:** U.S. President George W. Bush, on a visit to Albania, declares that Kosovo should be an independent country. **11 June:** UN Secretary-General Ban Ki-Moon expresses his support for the Ahtisaari Plan. **11 July:** President Fatmir Sejdiu and Prime Minister Agim Çeku visit Brussels for talks with EU Commission President Jose Barroso and Foreign Policy Representative

Javier Solana. **5 September:** Serbian State Secretary Dušan Proroković threatens a Serb military invasion if Kosovo declares its independence. **21 October:** Serb Defense Minister Dragan Šutanovac denies that plans are being made for a Serb invasion of Kosovo. **17 November:** Parliamentary elections, despite the low turnout, give victory to the Democratic Party (PDK) under Hashim Thaçi. The PDK wins 34.3 percent of the vote, the LDK 22.6 percent, the LDD and Christian-Democrats 10 percent, the Alliance for a New Kosovo (AKR) of Behgjet Pacolli 12.3 percent, the AAK 9.6 percent and the Ora initiative of Veton Surroi 4.1 percent. The seats in parliament are thus divided as follows: PDK 37, LDK 25, AKR 13, LDD 11, AAK 10, and the ethnic parties 24. The Serb minority boycott the elections again almost entirely.

Independence (2008-)

2008
3 January: The constituent assembly of the Kosovo parliament meets, with Hashim Thaçi of the PDK being elected to form a new government. **17 February:** The parliament of Kosovo declares the country's independence. **18 February:** The United States, the United Kingdom, France, Albania and Turkey recognize the new Republic of Kosovo. **20 February:** Germany recognizes the Republic of Kosovo. **21 February:** Italy, Denmark and Luxembourg recognizes the Republic of Kosovo. **27 February:** Kosovo Serb ministers in the Kosovo government resign in protest at independence; Switzerland recognizes the Republic of Kosovo. **28 February:** Austria recognizes the Republic of Kosovo.

4 March: Ireland and the Netherlands recognize the Republic of Kosovo. **17 March:** Unrest in northern Mitrovica results in the death of a Ukrainian policeman. **18 March:** Canada and Japan recognize the Republic of Kosovo. **19 March:** Croatia and Hungary recognize the Republic of Kosovo. **20 March:** Bulgaria recognizes the Republic of Kosovo. **3 April:** The Hague Tribunal finds Ramush Haradinaj innocent of war crimes. **8 April:** The United States opens an embassy in Prishtina. **9 April:** Parliament passes the new Kosovo Constitution that enters into force on 15 June. **28 June:** The Kosovo Serb community in northern Kosovo, supported by Belgrade, constitutes its own community assembly in Mitrovica. **11 July:** An EU donor conference in Brussels pledges 1.2 billion euros in aid for Kosovo. **21 July:** President Fatmir Sejdiu and Prime Minister Hashim Thaçi visit U.S. President Bush in Washington, D.C. **6 August:** Prime Minister Thaçi rejects UNMIK interference in police and customs administration. **27 August:** Kosovo opens its first 10 diplomatic missions abroad. **7 October:** Portugal recognizes the Republic of Kosovo. **8 October:** The UN General Assembly agrees to a request from Serbia to seek an advisory opinion on the legality of Kosovo's independence from the International Court of Justice in The Hague. **9 October:** Montenegro and Macedonia recognize the Republic of Kosovo. **10 October:** Former Finnish president and diplomat Martti Ahtissari wins the Nobel Peace Prize, in part for his role in resolving the Kosovo conflict. **11 November:** Kosovo government rejects the transfer of many competencies to the European Rule of Law Mission in Kosovo (EULEX) as incompatible with the country's sovereignty. **19 November:** Street protests in Prishtina against Serb conditions for the

EULEX mission. **25 November:** President Sejdiu and Prime Minister Thaçi reject proposal of UN Secretary-General Ban Ki-Moon for the EULEX mission. **December:** The transfer of rule of law functions from UNMIK to the Government of Kosovo. **9 December:** EULEX mission begins its work in Kosovo with ca. 1400 international legal experts.

2009
21 January: Creation of the Kosovo Security Force. **5 February:** Hundreds of Kosovo Serbs block the border to Serbia to protest against EULEX border checks. **19 March:** Spain, which has not recognized the Republic of Kosovo, unilaterally withdraws its troops from KFOR. **28 March:** Prime Minister Thaçi calls for the withdrawal of the UNMIK mission from Kosovo. **20 April:** Saudi Arabia is the first Arab country to recognize the Republic of Kosovo. **25 April:** Ethnic unrest in Mitrovica. **21 May:** U.S. Vice-President Joe Biden visits Kosovo. **31 May:** Prime Minister Hashim Thaçi and Albanian Prime Minister Sali Berisha open the Kalimash tunnel as the decisive segment of the new highway from Kosovo to Durrës on the Adriatic coast. **29 June:** Kosovo joins the International Monetary Fund and the World Bank. **25 August:** EULEX is the object of violent protests by the *Vetëvendosje* Movement, angered at police cooperation with Serbia in Kosovo. **18 September:** The Kosovo Security Force begins its work officially. **1 October:** Albanian President Sali Berisha visits Kosovo and speaks of national unification under the aegis of the European Union. **17 October:** Kosovo and Macedonia establish diplomatic relations. **1-2 November:** Former U.S. President Bill Clinton visits Prishtina. **15 November:**

Municipal elections in Kosovo give victory to the PDK in 15 municipalities, the LDK in seven, the AAK in seven and the Independent Liberal Party SLS in two. Kosovo Serbs are urged by Belgrade to boycott the vote, and do so in their vast majority in northern Kosovo. **1 December:** Upon the initiative of the Government of Serbia, the International Court of Justice in The Hague begins consultations for an advisory opinion on the legality of Kosovo's independence. **10 December:** The Kosovo Force announces a troop reduction from 14,000 to 10,000 men.

2010
20 March: Prime Minister Hashim Thaçi attends a meeting of western Balkan leaders at Brdo Castle in Slovenia, boycotted by Serbia. **1 April:** Cabinet shuffle in the Thaçi government, with the appointment of Edita Tahiri, Bujar Bukoshi and Bajram Rexhepi as new ministers. **21 July:** The Appeals Chamber of the Hague Tribunal reverses the Haradinaj Judgement and calls for a retrial. Ramush Haradinaj and his co-accused are detained once again in The Hague. **22 July:** The International Court of Justice in The Hague rules that Kosovo's declaration of independence in 2008 did not violate international law. **5 September:** Consecration of new Mother Teresa Catholic Church in Prishtina. **27 September:** Fatmir Sejdiu resigns as President of Kosovo following constitutional court decision. **13-14 October:** U.S. Secretary of State Hillary Clinton visits Kosovo. **29 October:** NATO announces its decision to reduce KFOR troops from 10,000 to 5,000. **2 November:** Parliament in Kosovo is dissolved after a vote of no confidence. **6 November:** The Mayor of Prishtina, Isa

Mustafa, is chosen as the new head of the LDK. **6 November:** Prishtina airport is renamed after Adem Jashari. **11 November:** Former speaker of parliament Nexhat Daci is convicted by a EULEX court of abuse of power. **12 December:** Parliamentary elections in Kosovo without a clear winner. The PDK wins 33.5 percent (36 seats) of the vote, the LDK 23.6 percent (26 seats), the *Vetëvendosja* Movement 12.2 percent (13 seats), and the AAK 10.8 percent (8 seats). The remaining 25 seats are reserved for the Kosovo Serbs and other ethnic minorities. **14 December:** Swiss politician and Council of Europe member Dick Marty accuses Hashim Thaçi of mafia contacts, of dealing in drugs and arms, and of other major crimes.

2011

3 February: Isa Mustafa leaves parliament and resumes office as mayor of Prishtina. **22 February:** The new parliament of Kosovo is constituted with Hashim Thaçi as prime minister, Enver Hoxhaj as foreign minister, and Jakup Krasniqi as speaker. **7 April:** Atifete Jahjaga elected as President of Kosovo, the first woman to hold this office. **2 July:** Cross-border travel agreement between Kosovo and Serbia. **25 July:** Clashes at two border crossings between Kosovo and Serbia over import regulations and subsequent closing of these crossings. **18 August:** Start of the retrial of Ramush Haradinaj at the ICTY in The Hague. **2 September:** Kosovo and Serbia reach an agreement in Brussels on customs. **16 September:** EULEX takes over two disputed border crossings in northern Kosovo. **19 September:** President Atifete Jahjaga, Prime Minister Hashim Thaçi and Deputy Prime Minister Behgjet Pacolli meet U.S. Secretary of State Hillary Clinton in New York.

27 September: Clashes in northern Kosovo between ethnic Serbs and KFOR. **9 November:** More clashes between ethnic Serbs and Albanians at the northern border crossing of Jarinje.

2012

6 January: Clashes in Deçan and Peja of Albanians protesting the visit there of Serbian President Boris Tadić. **14 January:** Consular agreement between Albania and Kosovo for mutual representation. **14 February:** Establishment of a national Anti-Corruption Council. **5 July:** Trade agreement between Kosovo and the EU. **9 September:** Achievement of full sovereignty and the end of the international monitoring of Kosovo's independence. **21 September:** According to the latest census, the population of Kosovo is 1,739,825. This figure does not include the Serbs of northern Kosovo who boycotted the census. **7 October:** According to further census information, 82,000 people in Kosovo above the age of ten are functionally illiterate. **22 October:** Clashes in Prishtina organised by the *Vetëvendosja* Movement to protest against negotiations between Kosovo and Serbia. **1 November:** EU Foreign Affairs Representative Catherine Ashton and U.S. Secretary of State Hillary Clinton visit Prishtina. **28 November:** Celebrations in Kosovo for the centenary of Albanian independence. **29 November:** Ramush Haradinaj acquitted again at the ICTY retrial in The Hague.

2013

13 January: The Serbian leadership elaborates a plan for the *de facto* independence of northern Kosovo. **18 January:** A provisional agreement is reached in

Brussels between Hashim Thaçi and the Serbian Prime Minister Ivica Dačić on customs duties at the northern border. **6 February:** President Jahjaga meets Serbian President Tomislav Nikolić in Brussels. **14 March:** Bedri Hamza is appointed as head of the National Bank of Kosovo. **19 April:** An agreement is reached between Kosovo and Serbia, after long negotiations, on substantial autonomy for northern Kosovo. **13 June:** The Co-operative Republic of Guyana in South America becomes the 100th foreign country to recognize Kosovo. **17 June:** Kosovo and Serbia exchange diplomatic representatives despite Serbia's continued unwillingness to recognise Kosovo as an independent state. **1 July:** A military agreement is signed between Kosovo and Albania. **10 July:** Parliament passes a controversial amnesty law on crimes committed during the Kosovo War. **13 September:** Albanian Prime Minister Edi Rama visits Kosovo following his electoral victory. **19 September:** A Lithuanian customs officer of the EULEX mission is killed by a Serb extremist in northern Kosovo. **29 October:** A study reveals that 2.6 percent of water samples taken in Kosovo are radioactive. **3 November:** Municipal elections in Kosovo. **26 December:** Shpend Ahmeti of the *Vetëvendosja* Movement replaces Isa Mustafa of the LDK as mayor of Prishtina.

2014
23 January: The European Parliament passes a resolution (485 to 94) calling for all EU member states to recognise Kosovo. **29 January:** Student protests take place in Prishtina calling for the resignation of university rector Ibrahim Gashi because of corruption. **23 April:** The Parliament of Kosovo agrees to the creation of a special

court to try one-time members of the KLA for organ trafficking. **7 May:** Dissolution of parliament and the call for new national elections. **8 June:** Parliamentary elections in Kosovo result in no clear winner, with the Democratic Party under Hashim Thaçi receiving 30.7 percent of the vote (37 seats), the LDK under Isa Mustafa 25.7 percent (30 seats), the *Vetëvendosja* Movement under Albin Kurti 13.5 percent (16 seats), the AAK 9.6 percent (11 seats), and the *Nisma* Initiative of Fatmir Limaj 5.2 percent (6 seats). **20 August:** The Minister of the Interior reports that over 30,000 Kosovars have given up their citizenship and taken on that of other countries because of continuing travel restrictions for Kosovo passport holders. **22 August**: Growing political crisis in Kosovo with no new government being formed after the June elections. **8 December:** Isa Mustafa of the LDK is finally elected as Prime Minister of Kosovo, in coalition with Hashim Thaçi of the Democratic Party who is made deputy prime minister and minister of foreign affairs.

BIBLIOGRAPHY
OF THE HISTORY OF KOSOVO

GENERAL HISTORY

Acin-Kosta, Miloš. *Branioci Kosova, 1389-1989* [The Defenders of Kosovo]. 2. dop. i pros. izd. Washington: Ravnogorski venac, 1989. xxxii + 470 pp.

Arsenijević, Vesna. *Kosovo: zemlja živih, 1389-1989* [Kosovo: Land of the Living, 1389-1989]. Belgrade: Manastir svetog Stefana, 1989.

Bartl, Peter. *Grundzüge der jugoslawischen Geschichte* [The Basics of Yugoslav History]. Darmstadt: Wissenschaftliche Buchgesellschaft, 1985. ix + 190 pp.

——. *Albanien: vom Mittelalter bis zur Gegenwart* [Albania: From the Middle Ages to the Present]. Südosteuropa-Gesellschaft. Regensburg, Germany: Friedrich Pustet, 1995. 304 pp.

Bataković, Dušan. *Kosovo i Metohija u srpsko-arbanaškim odnosima* [Kosovo and Metohija in Serbian-Albanian Relations]. Belgrade: Čigoja štampa, 2006. 393 pp.

Berisha, Ibrahim et al. *Serbian Colonization and Ethnic Cleansing in Kosova: Documents and Evidence*. Prishtina: Kosova Information Center, 1993. 102 pp.

Braha, Shaban. *Gjenocidi serbomadh dhe qëndresa shqiptare, 1844-1990* [Greater Serbian Genocide and Albanian Resistance, 1844-1990]. Gjakova: Lumi-T, 1991. 584 pp.

Castellan, Georges. *Histoire des Balkans (XIVe-XXe siècle)* [History of the Balkans (XIV-XX centuries)]. Paris: Fayard, 1991. 532 pp.

——. *History of the Balkans: From Mohammed the Conqueror to Stalin.* Translated from the French by Nicholas Bradley. East European Monographs, CCCXXV. Boulder, Colo.: East European Monographs, 1992. 493 pp.

——. *Histoire de l'Albanie et des Albanais* [History of Albania and the Albanians]. Crozon, France: Editions Armeline, 2002. 204 pp.

Chiari, Bernhard. *Kosovo: Wegweiser zur Geschichte* [Kosovo: Guide to History]. 3. Auflage. Paderborn: Schöningh, 2008. 276 pp.

Clark, Victoria. *Why Angels Fall: A Journey through Orthodox Europe from Byzantium to Kosovo.* New York: St. Martin's Press, 2000. 460 pp.

Destani, Bejtullah D. (ed.). *The Albanian Question.* London: Albanian Community Centre 'Faik Konica,' 1996. 54 pp.

——. *Albania & Kosovo: Political and Ethnic Boundaries, 1867-1946. Documents and Maps.* Farnham Common, Slough, England: Archive Editions, 1999. 1,100 pp.

Di Lellio, Anna. *The Battle of Kosovo: an Albanian Epic.* With translations by Robert Elsie. London: I. B. Tauris, 2009. 192 pp.

Djokic, Dejan (ed.). *Yugoslavism: Histories of a Failed Idea.* London: C. Hurst, 2002. x + 356 pp.

Doçi, Rexhep. *Antroponimia e shqiptarëve të Kosovës, 1* [Anthroponomy of the Kosovo Albanians, 1]. Prishtina: Instituti Albanologjik, 1990. 245 pp.

———. *Iliro-shqiptarët dhe serbët në Kosovë: sipas onomastikës* [The Illyro-Albanians and the Serbs in Kosovo: Onomastic Evidence]. Prishtina: Instituti Albanologjik, 1994. 345 pp.

Elsie, Robert. *Writing in Light: Early Photography of Albania and the Southwestern Balkans. Dritëshkronja: fotografia e hershme nga Shqipëria dhe Ballkani jugperëndimor.* Prishtina: ATV Media Company & Arbi Ltd, 2007. 311 pp.

———. *Albania and Kosova in Colour, 1913: the Autochromes of the Albert Kahn Collection. L'Albanie et le Kosovo en couleurs. Les autochromes de la Collections Albert Kahn. Shqipëria dhe Kosova në ngjyra 1913: autokromat e koleksionit Alber Kan.* Edited by Gerda Mulder & Richard van den Brink. Tirana: Skanderbeg Books, 2008. 105 pp.

———. *Fjalor historik i Kosovës* [Historical Dictionary of Kosovo]. Përktheu nga anglishtja Majlinda Nishku. Tirana: Skanderbeg Books, 2011. 436 pp.

———. *Historical Dictionary of Kosovo*, Second edition. Historical Dictionaries of Europe, No. 79. Lanham, Toronto, Plymouth: Scarecrow Press, 2010. lvi + 395 pp.

———. *Biographical Dictionary of Albanian History*. London: I. B. Tauris, in association with The Centre for Albanian Studies, 2013. ix + 541 pp.

Gallagher, Tom. *Outcast Europe: The Balkans, 1789-1989. From the Ottomans to Milošević.* London: Routledge, 2001. 336 pp.

Garašanin, Milutin (ed.). *Iliri i Albanci: serija predavanja održanih od 21. maja do 4. juna 1986. godine* [The Illyrians and the Albanians: Series of Lectures Held from 21 May to 4 June 1986]. Naučni skupovi, knjiga 39. Odeljenje istorijskih nauka, knjiga 10. *Les Illyriens et les Albanais. Série de conférences tenues du 21 mai au 4 juin 1986.* Colloques scientifiques, vol. 39, Classe des sciences historiques, vol. 10. Belgrade:

Srpska Akademija Nauka i Umetnosti/Académie Serbe des Sciences et des Arts, 1988. 375 pp.

Garde, Paul. *Vie et mort de la Yougoslavie* [Life and Death of Yugoslavia]. Paris: Fayard 1992, reprint 1994. 444 pp.

Hoxha, Sherafedin. *Shtypi i kombeve dhe i kombësive të Kosovës, 1871-1983* [The Press of the Peoples and Minorities of Kosovo, 1871-1983]. Prishtina: Rilindja, 1987. 240 pp.

Imami, Petrit. *Srbi i Albanci kroz vekove* [Serbs and Albanians through the Centuries]. Drugo dopunjeno izdanje. Belgrade: Samizdat FreeB92, 1999. 558 pp.

Ippen, Theodor Anton. *Novibazar und Kossovo–das alte Rascien: eine Studie* [Novi Pazar and Kosovo–Old Rascia: A Study]. Vienna: Alfred Hölder, 1892. 159 pp.

――. *Shqipëria e vjetër: Studime gjeografike, etnografike, historike nga ish-konsulli i përgjithshëm i monarkisë austro-hungareze në Shqipëri* [Old Albania: Geographical, Ethnographical and Historical Studies by the Former Austro-Hungarian Consul-General in Albania]. Seria albanologjike. Përkthyer nga origjinali Gjerak Karaiskaj, Ardian Klosi. Tirana: K&B, 2003. 272 pp.

Ismajli, Rexhep & Kraja, Mehmet (ed.). *Kosova: vështrim monografik* [Kosovo: A Monographic Survey]. Prishtina: Akademia e Shkencave dhe e Arteve e Kosovës, 2011. 646 pp.

――. *Kosova: A Monographic Survey*. Prishtina: Kosova Academy of Sciences and Arts, 2013. 508 pp.

Jacques, Edwin E. *The Albanians. An Ethnic History from Prehistoric Times to the Present*. Jefferson, N.C.: McFarland, 1995. 768 pp.

Jelavich, Barbara. *History of the Balkans*. 2 vol. Cambridge: Cambridge University Press, 1983. 416 & 476 pp.

Jelavich, Charles, and Barbara Jelavich. *The Balkans in Transition: Essays on the Development of Balkan Life and*

Politics since the Eighteenth Century. Berkeley: University of California Press, 1963; reprint 1974. 451 pp.

Jirecek, Constantin. *Geschichte der Serben* [History of the Serbs]. Geschichte der Europäischen Staaten, Nr. 38. 2 vol. Gotha: Friedrich Andreas Perthes, 1911, 1918. 442 + 228 pp.

Jovanović, Jovan. *Južna Srbija od kraja XVIII veka do oslobodjenja* [Southern Serbia from the End of the Eighteenth Century to Liberation]. Belgrade: Kon, 1938. 186 pp.

Judah, Tim. *The Serbs: History, Myth and the Destruction of Yugoslavia.* Third Edition. New Haven: Yale University Press, 2010. 368 pp.

Krestić, Vasilije, and Djordje Lekić. *Kosovo i Metohija tokom vekova* [Kosovo and Metohija over the Centuries]. Prishtina: Grigorije Božović, 1995. 401 pp.

Judah, Tim. *Kosovo: What Everyone Needs to Know.* Oxford: Oxford University Press, 2008. 184 pp.

Magaš, Branka. *The Destruction of Yugoslavia: Tracking the Break-up, 1980-1992.* London: Verso, 1993. 366 pp.

Malcolm, Noel. *Kosovo: A Short History.* London: Macmillan, 1998. 491 pp.

———. *Kosova: një histori e shkurtër* [Kosovo: A Short History]. Përkth. A. Karjagdiu. Prishtina: Koha, 1998. 506 pp.

———. *Kosovo: kratka povijest* [Kosovo: A Short History]. Sarajevo: Dani, 2000.

Métais, Serge. *Histoire des Albanais: des Illyriens à l'indépendance du Kosovo* [History of the Albanians: From the Illyrians to the Independence of Kosovo]. Paris: Fayard, 2006. 451 pp.

Mihailović, Kosta. *Kosovo and Metohija: Past, Present and Future. Belgrade*: Serbian Academy of Sciences and Art, 2006. 532 pp.

83

Pavlowitsch, Stevan K. *The Improbable Survivor: Yugoslavia and its Problems, 1918-1988.* London: Hurst, 1988. 167 pp.

——. *A History of the Balkans, 1804-1945.* London: Longman, 1999. 375 pp.

Petković, Ranko, and Gordana Filipović (ed.). *Kosovo: Past and Present.* Translated by Margot and Boško Milosavljević. Belgrade: Review of International Affairs, 1989. 384 pp.

Petranović, Branko. *Istorija Jugoslavije, 1918-1978* [History of Yugoslavia, 1918-1978]. Belgrade: Nolit, 1981. 648 pp.

Petrovich, Michael B. *A History of Modern Serbia.* 2 vol. New York: Harcourt Brace Jovanovich, 1976. 731 pp.

Pollo, Stefanaq, and Arben Puto (ed.). *Histoire de l'Albanie des origines à nos jours* [History of Albania from Its Origins to the Present Day]. Roanne: Horvath, 1974. 372 pp.

——. *The History of Albania from Its Origins to Present Day.* With the collaboration of Kristo Frashëri and Skënder Anamali. Translated from the French by Carol Wiseman, Ginnie Hole. London: Routledge & Kegan Paul. 1981. 322 pp.

Ristelhueber, René. *A History of the Balkan Peoples.* New York: Twayne, 1950. xviii + 470 pp.

Samardžić, Radovan. *Kosovo i Metohija u srpskoj istoriji* [Kosovo and Metohija in Serb History]. Belgrade: Srpska književna zadruga, 1989. 436 pp.

——. *Kosovo und Metohien in der serbischen Geschichte* [Kosovo and Metohija in Serb History]. Lausanne: L'Age d'Homme, 1989. 502 pp.

Samardžić, Radovan et al. *Kosovski boj u evropejskoj književnosti* [The Battle of Kosova in European Literature]. Belgrade: Srpska književna zadruga, 1994. 378 pp.

Samardžić, Radovan, Sima M. Ćirković, Olga Zirojević, Radmila Tričković, Dušan Bataković, Veselin Djuretić, Kosta

Čavoški, and Atanasije Jevtić. *Le Kosovo-Metohija dans l'histoire serbe* [Kosovo and Metohija in Serb History]. Lausanne: L'Age d'Homme, 1990. 350 pp.

Samim Visoka, Vasfi. *Shqipëria e vërtetë: Nëna Kosovë. Ndjenja dhe mendime. Përshtypje udhtimi nga Tokat e Liruara. Tiranë-Kosovë 1938- 1943* [True Albania: Mother Kosovo. Feelings and Thoughts. Impressions of a Trip Back from the Liberated Territories, Tirana-Kosovo, 1938-1943]. Tirana: Shtyp. e Shtetit, 1943. 144 pp.

Schevill, Ferdinand. *A History of the Balkans: From the Earliest Times to the Present Day.* New York: Dorset Press, 1991. viii + 558 pp.

Schmitt, Oliver Jens. *Kosovo: kurze Geschichte einer zentralbalkanischen Landschaft* [Kosovo: Short History of a Central Balkan Areal], Vienna: Böhlau, 2008. 393 pp.

Schmitt, Oliver Jens and Eva Frantz (ed.). *Albanische Geschichte: Stand und Perspektiven der Forschung* [Albanian History: State and Perspective of Research]. Südosteuropäische Arbeiten, 140. Munich: R. Oldenbourg, 2009. 280 pp.

Singleton, Frederick. *A Short History of the Yugoslav Peoples.* Cambridge: Cambridge University Press, 1985. 309 pp.

Slijepčević, Djoko M. *Srpsko-arbanaški odnosi kroz vekove sa posebnim osvrtom na novije vreme* [Serb-Albanian Relations through the Centuries, with Particular Attention to Recent Times]. Munich: Selbstverlag, 1974. 439 pp.

Stanković, Todor P. *Beleške o Staroj Srbiji i Maćedoniji* [Notes on Old Serbia and Macedonia]. Niš: Štamp. Kralj. Srbije, 1915. 194 pp.

Stanojević, Stanoje. *Istorija srpskoga naroda* [History of the Serb People]. Belgrade, 1908, reprint Belgrade: Prosveta, 1993. 431 pp.

Stavrianos, Leften Stavros. *The Balkans Since 1953.* New York: Rinehart, 1958, reprint 2000. 970 pp.

Stojančević, Vladimir. *Srbija i Albanci u XIX i početkom XX veka. Ciklus predavanja 10-25. novembar 1987* [Serbs and Albanians in the Nineteenth and Early Twentieth Centuries. Cycle of Lectures, 10-25 November 1987]. Belgrade: Srpska Akademija Nauka i Umetnosti, 1990. 311 pp.

Šufflay, Milan von. *Srbi i Arbanasi: njihova simbioza u sredjem vjeku* [Serbs and Albanians: Their Symbiosis in the Middle Ages]. Biblioteka Arhiva za Arbanasku Starinu, Jezik i Etnologiju. 1. Belgrade: Izdanje Seminaria za Arbanasku Filologiju, 1925; reprint 1991. 142 pp.

———. *Serbët dhe shqiptarët* [Serbs and Albanians]. Përkthyer prej sllavishtes nga Zef Fekeçi e Karl Gurakuqi. Tirana, 1926, reprint 1968. 238 pp.

Sugar, Peter F. *Southeastern Europe under Ottoman Rule, 1354-1804.* History of East Central Europe 5. Seattle, Wash.: University of Washington Press, 1977. 384 pp.

Terzić, Slavenko (ed.). *Response to Noel Malcolm's Book "Kosovo: A Short History." Scientific Discussion on Noel Malcolm's Book "Kosovo: A Short History" (Macmillan, London 1998). 8th October 1999.* With Milorad Ekmečić, Djordje Janković, Ema Miljković-Bojanić, Slavenko Terzić, Mile Bjelajac, Djordje Borozan, Ljubodrag Dimić. Editor in Chief Slavenko Terzić. Institute of History of the Serbian Academy of Sciences and Arts, Collections of Works, Volume 18. Belgrade: SANU, 2000. 193 pp.

Thëngjilli, Petrika. *Historia e popullit shqiptar, 395-1875* [History of the Albanian People, 395-1875]. Tirana: Shtëpia Botuese e Librit Universitar, 1999. 453 pp.

Todorova, Maria. *Balkan Identities: Nation and Memory*. New York: New York University Press, 2004. 374 pp.

Verli, Marenglen. *Reforma agrare kolonizuese në Kosovë* [Colonialist Agrarian Reform in Kosovo]. Akademia e Shkencave të Republikës së Shqipërisë. Tirana: Iliria, Tirana 1991. 215 pp.

——. *Shfrytëzimi ekonomik i Kosovës, 1970-1990* [The Economic Exploitation of Kosovo, 1970-1990]. Tirana: Dituria, 1994. 125 pp.

——. *Kosova në fokusin e historisë: studime, analiza, dokumente* [Kosovo in the Focus of History: Studies, Analyses, Documents], 2 vol. Tirana: Botimpex, 2002, 2003. 407 & 320 pp.

ARCHAEOLOGY, PREHISTORY
AND ANCIENT HISTORY

Boardmann, J., I. E. S. Edwards, N. G. L. Hammond, and E. Sollberger (ed.). *The Prehistory of the Balkans, and the Middle East and the Aegean World. Tenth to Eighth Centuries BC.* Cambridge Ancient History, 2nd Edition, vol. III, pt. 1. Cambridge: Cambridge University Press, 1982.

Ceka, Neritan. *Ilirët* [The Illyrians]. Tirana: Shtëpia Botuese e Librit Universitar, 2000. 334 pp.

——. *The Illyrians to the Albanians*. Translation Benet Koleka. Tirana: Migjeni, 2005. 394 pp.

Ceka, Neritan, and Muzafer Korkuti. *Arkeologjia: Greqia, Roma, Iliria* [Archeology: Greece, Rome, Illyria]. Tirana: Soros, 1993, reprint 1998. 423 pp.

Čerškov, Emil. *Rimljani u Kosovu i Metohiji* [The Romans in Kosovo und Metohija]. Belgrade: Arheološko Društvo Jugoslavije, 1969. 139 pp.

———. *Municipium DD*. Prishtina: Muzej Kosovo & Belgrade: Arheološko Društvo Jugoslavije, 1970.

Evans, Arthur John. Antiquarian Researches in Illyricum. in: *Archaeologia*, Westminster, 48 (1885), p. 1-105; 49 (1886), p. 1-167.

———. *Ancient Illyria: an Archaeological Exploration*. Introduction by John Wilkes. Edited by Bejtullah Destani. London: I. B. Tauris in association with the Centre for Albanian Studies, 2006. 192 pp.

Ferri, Naser. *Monumentet ushtarake të periudhës romake në Mezi të Epërme* [Military Monuments of the Roman Period in Upper Moesia]. Peja: Dukagjini, 2001. 385 pp.

Garašanin, Milutin (ed.). *Iliri i Albanci: serija predavanja održanih od 21. maja do 4. juna 1986. godine* [The Illyrians and the Albanians: Series of Lectures Held from 21 May to 4 June 1986]. Naučni skupovi, knjiga 39. Odeljenje istorijskih nauka, knjiga 10. *Les Illyriens et les Albanais. Série de conférences tenues du 21 mai au 4 juin 1986.* Colloques scientifiques, vol 39, Classe des sciences historiques, vol. 10. Belgrade: Srpska Akademija Nauka i Umetnosti/Académie Serbe des Sciences et des Arts, 1988. 375 pp.

Kanitz, Felix Philipp. Römische Studien in Serbien [Roman Studies in Serbia], Vienna, 1892.

Mirdita, Zef. *Religjioni dhe kultet e Dardanëve dhe Dardanisë në antikë* [The Religion and the Cults of the Dardanians and of Dardania in Ancient Times]. Zagreb: Unioni i Bashkësive Shqiptare në Republikën e Kroacisë, 2001. 208 pp.

Papazoglu, Fanula (= Papazoglou, Fanoula). *Srednobalkanska plemena u prerimsko doba: Tribali, Autarijati, Dardanci, Skordisci i Mezi* [Central Balkan Tribes in Pre-Roman Times. Triballi, Autariatae, Dardanians, Scordisci and Moesians]. Sarajevo: Akademija Nauka u Umjetnosti Bosne i Hercegovine, 1969. 496 pp.

——. *Central Balkan Tribes in Pre-Roman Times. Triballi, Autariatae, Dardanians, Scordisci and Moesians.* Translated by Mary Stanfield-Popović. Amsterdam: Adolf M. Hakkert, 1978. 664 pp.

Përzhita, Luan, Kemajl Luci, Gëzim Hoxha, Adem Bunguri, Fatmir Peja, and Tomor Kastrati (ed.). *Harta arkeologjike e Kosovës. Archaeological Map of Kosova.* Vol. 1. Prishtina: Akademia e Shkencave dhe e Arteve e Kosovës, 2006. x + 394 pp.

Shukriu, Edi. *Dardania paraurbane: studime arkeologjike të Kosovës* [Pre-urban Dardania: Archeological Studies of Kosovo]. Peja: Dukagjini, 1996. 242 pp.

Stipčević, Aleksandar. *The Illyrians: History and Culture.* Translated from Serbo-Croatian by S. Burton. Park Bridge, N.J.: Noyes Press, 1977. 291 pp.

——. *Iliri: povijest, život, kultura* [The Illyrians: History, Life, Culture]. Zagreb: Školska knjiga, 1991. 203 pp.

Wilkes, John. *The Illyrians.* Oxford: Blackwell, 1992. 351 pp.

PRE-TWENTIETH CENTURY HISTORY

Abdyli, Tahir. *Hasan Prishtina në lëvizjen kombëtare e demokratike shqiptare 1908-1933* [Hasan Prishtina in the

89

Albanian National and Democratic Movement 1908-1933].
Prishtina: GME, 2003. 390 pp.

Bajrami, Hakif. *Politika e shfarosjes së shqiptarëve dhe kolonizimi serb i Kosovës, 1844-1995* [The Policy of the Extermination of the Albanian and the Serb Colonization of Kosovo, 1844-1995]. Prishtina: Qendra për Informim e Kosovës, 1995. 207 pp.

———. *Kosova: njëzetë shekuj të identitetit të saj. Argumente historike.* [Kosovo: Twenty Centuries of its Identity. Historical Arguments]. Prishtina: Era, 2001. 156 pp.

Bartl, Peter. *Die albanischen Muslime zur Zeit des nationalen Unabhängigkeitsbewegung 1878-1912* [The Albanian Muslims at the Time of the National Independence Movement 1878-1912]. Albanische Forschungen 8. Wiesbaden, Germany: Harrassowitz, 1968. 207 pp.

———. *Der Westbalkan zwischen spanischer Monarchie und osmanischem Reich. Zur Türkenproblematik an der Wende vom 16. zum 17. Jahrhundert* [The Western Balkans between the Spanish Monarchy and the Ottoman Empire. On the Turkish Problem at the Turn of the 16th to 17th Centuries]. Albanische Forschungen 14. Wiesbaden, Germany: Harrassowitz, 1974. 258 pp.

———. *Quellen und Materialien zur albanischen Geschichte im 17. und 18. Jahrhundert* [Sources and Material on Albanian History in the 17th and 18th Centuries]. 2 Vol. Albanische Forschungen 15 & 20. Wiesbaden, Germany: Harrassowitz, 1975/Munich: Trofenik, 1979. 135 & 257 pp.

Baxhaku, Fatos, and Karl Kaser. *Die Stammesgesellschaften Nordalbaniens. Berichte und Forschungen österreichischer Konsuln und Gelehrter (1861-1917)* [The Tribal Societies of

Northern Albania. Reports and Research by Austrian Consuls and Scholars (1861-1917)]. Vienna: Böhlau, 1996. 459 pp.

Belegu, Xhafer. *Lidhja e Prizrenit e veprimet e sajë, 1878-1881* [The League of Prizren and Its Activities, 1878-1881]. Tirana: Kristo Luarasi, 1939. 199 pp.

Bizzi, Marino: "The Archbishop of Bar Taken Hostage in Albania, 1610." In *Early Albania: A Reader of Historical Texts, 11th-17th Centuries*, ed. Robert Elsie. Balkanologische Veröffentlichungen, Band 39. Wiesbaden: Harrassowitz, 2003. pp. 77-129.

Blumi, Isa. *Redefining Balkan Nationalism: Albanian Identities at the End of the Ottoman Empire.* London: I. B. Tauris, 2010.

Boban, Vladimir. *Jastrebov u Prizrenu: kulturno-prosvetne prilike u Prizrenu i rad ruskog konzula I. S. Jastrebova u drugoj polovini devetnaestog veka* [Jastrebov in Prizren: Cultural and Educational Conditions in Prizren and the Work of the Russian Consul I. S. Jastrebov in the Second Half of the Nineteenth Century]. Prishtina: Jedinstvo, 1983. 268 pp.

Braun, Maximilian. *Kosovo: die Schlacht auf dem Amselfelde in geschichtlicher und epischer Überlieferung* [Kosovo: The Battle of Kosovo in Historical and Epic Tradition]. Slavisch-baltische Quellen und Forschungen, 8. Leipzig, 1937.

Brestovci, Sadulla. *Marrëdhëniet shqiptare-serbo-malazeze, 1830-1878* [Albanian-Serbian-Montenegrin Relations, 1830-1878]. Prishtina: Instituti Albanologjik, 1983. 291 pp.

Ćidić, L., and D. Lazić (ed.). *Očevici o velikoj seobi srba* [Eye-Witnesses to the Great Migration of the Serbs], Kruševac, 1990.

Clayer, Nathalie. *Aux origines du nationalisme albanais: la naissance d'une nation majoritairement musulmane en Europe* [To the Sources of Albanian Nationalism: The Birth of a Mostly Muslim Nation in Europe]. Paris: Karthala, 2007. 794 pp.

91

Čubrilović, Vasa. *Istorija političke misli u Srbiji XIX veka* [The History of Political Thought in Serbia in the Nineteenth Century]. Belgrade: Prosveta, 1958. 578 pp.

Dankoff, Robert, and Robert Elsie. *Evliya Çelebi in Albania and Adjacent Regions (Kosovo, Montenegro, Ohrid).* The Relevant Sections of the Seyahatname edited with Translation, Commentary and Introduction by Robert Dankoff and Robert Elsie. Evliya Çelebi's Book of Travels. Land and People of the Ottoman Empire in the Seventeenth Century. A Corpus of Partial Editions, vol. 5. Edited by Klaus Kreiser. Leiden, The Netherlands: E. J. Brill, 2000. 307 pp.

Dinić, Mihailo J. *Za istoriju rudarstva u srednjovekovnoj Serbiji i Bosni* [On the History of Mining in Medieval Serbia and Bosnia]. Posebna Izdanija, 240. 2 vol. Belgrade: Akademija Nauka, 1955, 1964. 109, 102 pp.

Elsie, Robert. *Early Albania: A Reader of Historical Texts, 11th-17th Centuries.* Balkanologische Veröffentlichungen, Band 39. Wiesbaden: Harrassowitz, 2003. ix + 233 pp.

Emmert, Thomas Allan. *Serbian Golgotha: Kosovo 1389.* East European Monographs, 277. Boulder: East European Monographs, 1990. 240 pp.

Evans, Arthur John. *Albanian Letters: Nationalism, Independence and the Albanian League.* London: I. B. Tauris, 2009. 224 pp.

Evliya, Efendi (= Evliya Çelebi, Aulija Çelebi). *Evliya Çelebi in Albania and Adjacent Regions (Kosovo, Montenegro, Ohrid).* The Relevant Sections of the Seyahatname edited with translation, commentary and introduction by Robert Dankoff and Robert Elsie. Evliya Çelebi's Book of Travels. Land and People of the Ottoman Empire in the Seventeenth Century. A

Corpus of Partial Editions, edited by Klaus Kreiser. Volume 5. Leiden, New York, Cologne: E. J. Brill, 2000. 307 pp.

Faensen, Johannes. *Die albanische Nationalbewegung* [The Albanian National Movement]. Osteuropa-Institut an der Freien Universität Berlin. Balkanologische Veröffentlichungen 4. Berlin: In Kommission Harrassowitz, Wiesbaden, 1980. 195 pp.

Fine, John Van Antwerp. *The Early Medieval Balkans: A Critical Survey from the Sixth to the Late Twelfth Century.* Ann Arbor: University of Michigan Press, 1983.

———. *The Late Medieval Balkans: A Critical Survey from the Late 12th Century up to the Ottoman Conquest.* Ann Arbor: University of Michigan Press, 1987, reprint 1990. 699 pp.

Frashëri, Kristo. *Lidhja shqiptare e Prizrenit, 1878-1881* [The Albanian League of Prizren, 1878-1881]. Tirana: Toena, 1997. 509 pp.

Gawrych, George Walter. *The Crescent and the Eagle: Ottoman Rule, Islam and the Albanians, 1874 to 1913.* London: I. B. Tauris, 2006. 272 pp.

Gegaj, Athanase. *L'Albanie et l'invasion turque au XVe siècle* [Albania and the Turkish Invasion of the 15th Century]. Louvain, Belgium: Geuthner, 1937. 169 pp.

Gjini, Gaspër. *Skopsko-prizrenska biskupija kroz stoleća* [The Skopje-Prizren Diocese through the Centuries]. Zagreb: Kršćanska Sadašnjost, 1986. 240 pp.

———. *The Shkup-Prizren Diocese through Centuries.* Translated by Avni Spahiu. Prizren, Kosovo: Drita, 1999. ca. 280 pp.

Gopčević, Spiridion. *Oberalbanien und seine Liga: ethnographisch-politisch-historisch geschildert* [Upper Albania and Its League: Described from an Ethnographic,

Political and Historical Point of View]. Leipzig: Pierersche Hofbuchdruckerei, 1881. 586 pp.

——. *Makedonien und Alt-Serbien* [Macedonia and Old Serbia]. Mit 67 Original-Illustrationen und einer ethnographischen Karte. Vienna: L. W. Seidel, 1889. 512 pp.

——. *Stara Srbija i Makedonija* [Old Serbia and Macedonia]. Belgrade: Dimitrijevič, 1890.

Hadži-Vasiljević, Jovan. *Pitanje o Staroj Srbiji i skopljansko vladičansko pitanje* [The Question of Old Serbia and the Question of the Diocese of Skopje]. Belgrade: Jocković, 1902. 111 pp.

——. *Arnautski pokreti u XIX veku* [The Albanian Movement in the Nineteenth Century]. Belgrade: Davidović, 1905. 66 pp.

Ibrahimi, Nexhat. *Kontaktet e para të Islamit me popujt ballkanikë në periudhën paraosmane* [The Initial Contracts of Islam with the Peoples' of the Balkans in the Pre-Ottoman Period]. Skopje: Logos-A, 1997. 100 pp.

——. *Islami në trojet iliro-shqiptare gjatë shekujve* [Islam on Illyrian-Albanian Land for Centuries]. Skopje: Logos-A, 1999. 298 pp.

Islami, Myslim. *Lidhja shqiptare e Prizrenit dhe çështja e bashkimit kombëtar* [The Albanian League of Prizren and the Issue of National Unity]. Tirana: Afërdita, 1998. 499 pp.

Jovanović, Jovan. *Južna Srbija od kraja XVIII veka do oslobodjenja* [Southern Serbia from the End of the Eighteenth Century to Liberation]. Belgrade: Kon, 1938. 186 pp.

Mataj, Qemal. *Ymer Prizreni, 1829-1887: themelues i shtetit të parë autonom shqiptar* [Ymer Prizreni, 1829-1887: Founder of the First Autonomous Albanian State]. Prizren: s.e., 2002. 351 pp.

Melville, Ralphm and Hans-Jürgen Schröder (ed.). *Der Berliner Kongress von 1878: die Politik der Großmächte und die Probleme der Modernisierung in Südosteuropa in der zweiten Hälfte des 19. Jahrhunderts* [The Congress of Berlin of 1878: The Policies of the Great Powers and the Problems of Modernization in Southeast Europe in the Second Half of the Nineteenth Century]. Veröffentlichungen des Instituts für Europäische Geschichte Mainz. Abteilung Universalgeschichte, Beiheft 7. Wiesbaden: Franz Steiner, 1982. 539 pp.

Miller, William. *The Ottoman Empire and Its Successors, 1801-1927, with an Appendix, 1927-1936.* Cambridge: Cambridge University Press, 1936. 644 pp.

———. *Essays on the Latin Orient.* Amsterdam: Adolf M. Hakkert, 1964, reprint 1981. 582 pp.

Mihaljčić, Rade. *The Battle of Kosovo in History and in Popular Tradition.* Belgrade: Beogradski izdavačko-grafički zavod, 1989. 247 pp.

———. *Boj na Kosovu: starija i novije saznanja* [The Battle of Kosovo: Old and New Knowledge]. Belgrade: Izdavačka kuća književne novine, 1992. 618 pp.

Mikić, Djordje. *Društvene i ekonomske prilike kosovskih Srba u XIX i početkom XX veka* [Social and Economic Conditions of the Kosovo Serbs in the Nineteenth and Early Twentieth Centuries]. Belgrade: Srpska Akademija Nauka i Umetnosti, 1988. viii + 343 pp.

Mistrić, Slobodan Radojev. *Boj na Kosovu* [The Battle of Kosovo]. Amsterdam: L'atelier de la liberté, 1999. 166 pp.

Nikolajević, Milivoj J. *Severna Stara Srbija: vojno-geografska i istorijska studija* [Northern Old Serbia: A Military

95

Geographical and Historical Study]. Belgrade: Kraljevsko-srpska državna štamparija, 1892. iv + 120 pp.

Novaković, R. "O nekim pitanjima područja današnje Metohije krajem XII i početkom XIII veka" [On Some Issues of Territory in Modern Metohija at the End of the Twelfth and Beginning of the Thirteenth Centuries]. In *Zbornik Radova Vizantološkog Instituta*, 9 (1966). pp. 195-215.

Peruničić, Branko. *Zulumi aga i begova u kosovskom vilajetu, 1878-1913* [Acts of Violence of the Agas and Beys in the Vilayet of Kosovo, 1878-1913]. Belgrade: Nova knjiga, 1989. 670 pp.

Pirraku, Muhamet. *Kultura kombëtare shqiptare deri në Lidhjen e Prizrenit* [Albanian National Culture up to the League of Prizren]. Prishtina: Instituti Albanologjik, 1989. 604 pp.

Pirraku, Muhamet (ed.). *Dritë e re për kryetarin e parë të Shqipërisë etnike: tribunë shkencore në 115-vjetorin e martirizimit të Ymer Prizrenit, 12 qershor 1887 - 12 qershor 2002* [New Light on the First Leader of Ethnic Albania: Scholarly Conference on the 115th Anniversary of the Death of Ymer Prizreni, 12 June 1887 - 12 June 2002]. Prishtina: Instituti Albanologjik, Dega e Historisë, 2002. 208 pp.

Pllana, Emin. *Kosova dhe reformat në Turqi, 1839-1912* [Kosovo and the Reforms in Turkey, 1839-1912]. Prishtina: Enti i historisë së Kosovës, 1978. 300 pp.

Pollo, Stefanaq, and Selami Pulaha. *Akte të Rilindjes kombëtare shqiptare, 1878-1912: memorandume, vendime, protesta, thirrje* [Acts of the Albanian National Revival, 1878-1912. Memoranda, Resolutions, Protests, Notifications]. Tirana: Akademia e Shkencave, 1978. 286 pp.

Popović, Dušan. *Velika seoba Srba 1690: Srbi seljaci i plemići* [The Great Migration of the Serbs, 1690: Serbs, Peasants and Noblemen]. Belgrade: Srpska književna Zadruga, 1954. 378 pp.

Popović, Janićije. *Život Srba na Kosovu 1812-1912* [Life of the Serbs in Kosovo, 1812-1912]. Belgrade: Književne novine, 1987. 400 pp.

Prifti, Kristaq. *Lidhja shqiptare e Prizrenit në dokumentet osmane, 1878-1881* [The Albanian League of Prizren in Ottoman Documents, 1878-1881]. Tirana: Akademia e Shkencave, 1978. 288 pp.

――. *Lidhja shqiptare e Pejës: lëvizja kombëtare, 1896-1900* [The Albanian League of Peja: The National Movement, 1896-1900]. Tirana: Akademia e Shkencave, 1984, reprint 2002. 448 pp.

――. *Le mouvement national albanais de 1896 à 1900: La Ligue de Peje* [The Albanian National Movement from 1896 to 1900: The League of Peja]. Tirana: Académie des Sciences, 1989. 296 pp.

Pulaha, Selami, and Kristaq Prifti (ed.). *La ligue albanaise de Prizren 1878-1881: Documents, 1* [The Albanian League of Prizren, 1878-1881: Documents, 1]. Tirana: Académie des Sciences, 1988. 474 pp.

Purković, Miodrag. *Istorija Srba: politička i kulturna istorija srednjega veka, do pade Zete, 1499* [History of the Serbs: Political and Cultural History of the Middle Ages up to the Fall of Zeta, 1499]. Belgrade: Evro, 1997. 230 pp.

Radojčić, N. (ed.). *Zakonik cara Stefana Dušana 1349 i 1354* [The Legal Code of Tsar Stephan Dushan, 1349 and 1354]. Belgrade, 1960. 176 pp.

Rahimi, Shukri. *Vilajeti i Kosovës më 1878-1912* [The Vilayet of Kosovo in 1878-1912]. Prishtina: Enti i teksteve, 1969. 209 pp.

———. *Gjurmime historike të Rilindjes kombëtare* [Historical Research into the National Awakening]. Prishtina: Instituti Albanologjik, 1986. 396 pp.

Rizaj, Skënder. *Kosova gjatë shekujve XV, XVI dhe XVII: administrimi, ekonomia, shoqëria dhe lëvizja popullore* [Kosovo in the Fifteenth, Sixteenth and Seventeenth Centuries: Administration, Economy, Society and the Popular Movement]. Tirana: 8 Nëntori, 1987. 501 pp.

———. *Dokumente angleze mbi lidhjen shqiptare të Prizrenit dhe fillimin e copëtimit të Ballkanit (1877-1885)/English documents on the Albanian League of Prizren and the start of the disintegration of the Balkans (1877-1885).* 2 vol. Prishtina: Rilindja, 1996. 285 + 423 pp.

Runciman, Stephen. *A History of the First Bulgarian Empire*. London: G. Bell, 1930. xii + 337 pp.

Skendi, Stavro. *Albanian National Awakening (1878-1912).* Princeton, N.J.: Princeton University Press, 1967. 498 pp.

Soulis, George Christos. *The Serbs and Byzantium during the Reign of Tsar Stephen Dušan (1331-1355) and his Successors.* Dumbarton Oaks Library and Collections: Washington 1984, reprint Athens, 1995. xxvi + 353 pp.

Stadtmüller, Georg. *Forschungen zur albanischen Frühgeschichte* [Research into Early Albanian History]. Zweite erweiterte Auflage. Albanische Forschungen 2. Wiesbaden, Germany: Harrassowitz, 1966. 221 pp.

Stojančević, Vladimir. *Jugoslovenski narodi u osmanskom carstvu od jedrenskog mira 1829. do pariskog kongresa 1856. godine* [The Peoples of Yugoslavia under Ottoman Rule from

the Treaty of Adrianople, 1829, to the Congress of Paris 1856].
Belgrade, 1971.

Tërnava, Muhamet. *Popullsia e Kosovës gjatë shekujve XIV-XVI* [The Population of Kosovo during the XIV-XVI Centuries]. Prishtina: Instituti Albanologjik, 1995. 491 pp.

———. *Studime për mesjetën* [Studies on the Middle Ages]. Peja: Dukagjini, 2000. 280 pp.

Thëngjilli, Petrika. *Kryengritjet popullore në vitet 30 të shekullit XIX: dokumente osmane* [Popular Uprisings in the '30s of the Nineteenth Century: Ottoman Documents]. Tirana: Akademia e Shkencave, 1978. 853 pp.

Uka, Sabit. *Shpërngulja e shqiptarëve nga Serbia jugore më 1877-1878 dhe vendosja e tyre në rrafshin e Kosovës* [The Displacement of Albanians from Southern Serbia in 1877-1878 and Their Settlement on the Plain of Kosovo]. Prishtina: Zëri, 1991.

———. *Dëbimi i shqiptarëve nga Sanxhaku i Nishit dhe vendosja e tyre ne Kosovë, 1878-1912* [The Expulsion of the Albanians from the Sandjak of Nish and Their Settlement in Kosovo, 1878-1912]. 2 vol. Prishtina: Valton, 1994. 300 & 339 pp.

Urošević, Atanasije. *Etnički procesi na Kosovu tokom turske vladavine* [Ethnic Processes in Kosovo during the Course of Turkish Rule]. Belgrade: Srpska Akademija Nauka i Umetnosti, 1987. viii + 112 pp.

Vucinich, Wayne S. *Kosovo: Legacy of a Medieval Battle.* A Modern Greek Studies Yearbook, Supplement, 1. Minnesota Mediterranean and East European Monographs. Minneapolis: University of Minnesota, 1991. xiii + 342 pp.

Xoxi, Koli. *Lidhja shqiptare e Prizrenit, 1878-1881* [The Albanian League of Prizren, 1878-1881]. Tirana: 8 Nëntori, 1978. 190 pp.

Zajmi, Tahir. *Lidhja e Prizrenit dhe lufta heroike e popullit për mbrojtjen e Kosovës* [The League of Prizren and the Heroic Struggle for the Defense of Kosovo]. Brussels, 1964. 126 pp.

Živković, Tibor, S. Bojanin and V. Petrović (ed.). *Selected Charters of Serbian Rulers (XII-XV Century), Relating to the Territory of Kosovo and Metohia.* Athens: Centre for Studies of Byzantine Civilisation, 2000. 151 pp.

TWENTIETH AND TWENTY-FIRST CENTURY HISTORY

Abdyli, Tahir. *Hasan Prishtina në lëvizjen kombëtare e demokratike shqiptare, 1908-1933* [Hasan Prishtina in the Albanian National and Democratic Movement, 1908-1933]. Prishtina: GME, 2003. 390 pp.

Andrić, Ivo. "Elaborat Ive Andrića o Albaniji iz 1939 godine" [Draft of Ivo Andrić on Albania from the Year 1939]. Bogdan Krizman (ed.). In *Časopis za suvremenu povijest,* Zagreb, 9 (1977), 2. pp. 77-89.

——. "Draft on Albania, 1939." In *Gathering Clouds: The Roots of Ethnic Cleansing in Kosovo and Macedonia. Early Twentieth-Century Documents.* Compiled, translated and edited by Robert Elsie. Dukagjini Balkan Books. Peja: Dukagjini, 2002. pp. 131-148.

Askew, Alice, and Claude Askew. *A Stricken Land: Serbia as We Saw It.* London: Eveleigh Nash, 1916. xvi + 363 pp.

Bajrami, Hakif. *Rrethanat shoqërore dhe politike në Kosovë më 1918-1941* [Social and Political Situation in Kosovo in 1918-1941]. Prishtina: Instituti i Historisë së Kosovës, 1981. 363 pp.

———. *Politika e shfarosjes së shqiptarëve dhe kolonizimi serb i Kosovës, 1844-1995* [The Policy of the Extermination of the Albanian and the Serb Colonization of Kosovo, 1844-1995]. Prishtina: Qendra për Informim e Kosovës, 1995. 207 pp.

———. *Dëbimi dhe shpërngulja e shqiptarëve në Turqi* [The Expulsion and Exile of the Albanians to Turkey]. Prishtina: Shoqata për Kthimin e Shqiptarëve të Shpërngulur nga Trojet e Veta, 1996. 505 pp.

———. *Politika serbe për rikolonizimin e Kosovës me sllavë, 1945-1948* [The Serb Policy for the Recolonization of Kosovo with Slavs, 1945-1948]. Prishtina: Era, 2002. 634 pp.

Balkanicus (= Protić, Stojan). *Das albanische Problem und die Beziehungen zwischen Serbien und Österreich-Ungarn* [The Albanian Problem and the Relations between Serbia and Austria-Hungary]. Von Balkanicus (pseud.). Ins Deutsche übertragen von Dr. jur. L. Markowitsch. Leipzig: O. Wigand, 1913. 104 pp.

———. *Albanski problem i Srbija i Austro-Ugarska* [The Albanian Problem and Serbia and Austria-Hungary]. Belgrade: Izdav. knjižarnica Gece Kona, 1913. 111 pp.

———. *Le problème albanais: la Serbie et l'Autriche-Hongrie.* [The Albanian Problem: Serbia and Austria-Hungary]. Paris: A. Challamel, 1913. 84 pp.

Banac, Ivo. *The National Question in Yugoslavia: Origins, History, Politics.* Ithaca, New York: Cornell University Press, 1984. 452 pp.

———. *Nacionalno pitanje u Jugoslaviji: porijeklo, povijest, politika* [The National Question in Yugoslavia: Origins, History, Politics]. Preveo s engleskoj. Zagreb: Globus, 1988. 420 pp.

——. *With Stalin Against Tito: Cominformist Splits in Yugoslav Communism.* Ithaca, New York: Cornell University Press, 1988. 294 pp.

Bisaku, Jean, Etienne Kurti, and Louis Gashi. *La situation de la minorité albanaise en Yugoslavie: mémoire présenté à la Société des Nations* [The Situation of the Albanian Minority in Yugoslavia: Memorandum Presented to the League of Nations]. Geneva, 1930. 43 pp.

——. "The Situation of the Albanian Minority in Yugoslavia. Memorandum Presented to the League of Nations." In *Gathering Clouds: The Roots of Ethnic Cleansing in Kosovo and Macedonia. Early Twentieth-Century Documents.* Compiled, translated and edited by Robert Elsie. Dukagjini Balkan Books. Peja: Dukagjini, 2002. pp. 47-96.

Bislimi, Daut. *Formacionet politiko-ushtarake në Kosovë, 1941-1945* [Political and Military Formations in Kosovo, 1941-1945]. Prishtina: Institut Albanologjik, 1997. 282 pp.

Bojović, Petar. *Odbrana Kosovoga Polja 1915 g. i zaštita odstupanija srpske vojske preko Albanije i Crne Gore* [The Defense of Kosovo Polje in 1915 and the Tactical Retreat of the Serbian Army through Albania and Montenegro]. Belgrade: Hipnos, 1990. 105 pp.

Braha, Shaban. *Idriz Seferi në lëvizjet kombëtare shqiptare* [Idriz Seferi and the Albanian National Movements]. Tirana: 8 Nëntori, 1981. 272 pp.

Bulatović, Liljana. *Prizrenski proces* [The Prizren Trial]. Novi Sad: Zajednica Novog Sada, 1988.

Cabanes, Pierre, and Bruno Cabanes. *Passions albanaises: de Berisha au Kosovo* [Albanian Passions: From Berisha to Kosovo]. Paris: Odile Jacob, 1998. 280 pp.

Cana, Zekeria. *Lëvizja kombëtare shqiptare në Kosovë, 1908-1912* [The Albanian National Movement in Kosovo, 1908-1912]. Prishtina: Rilindja, 1979, reprint 1982. 318 pp.

——. *Dimitrije Tucoviqi: koha dhe vepra* [Dimitrije Tucović: Time and Works]. Prishtina: Rilindja, 1983. 334 pp.

——. *Socialdemokracia serbe dhe çështje shqiptare, 1903-1914* [Serbian Social Democracy and the Albanian Question, 1903-1914]. Prishtina: Instituti Albanologjik, 1986. 376 pp.

——. *Populli shqiptar në kapërcyell të shekullit XX* [The Albanian People across the Twentieth Century]. Prishtina: Instituti Albanologjik, 1990. 342 pp.

Çeku, Ethem. *Mendimi politik i lëvizjes ilegale në Kosovë, 1945-1981* [The Political Thinking of the Illegal Movement in Kosovo, 1945-1981]. Prishtina: Brezi '81, 2003. 405 pp.

Çitaku, Ibrahim. *Azem Galica dhe veprimtaria luftarake e çetave kaçake të Drenicës* [Azem Galica and the Military Activity of the Kaçak Bands of Drenica]. Prishtina: 1996. 549 pp.

Čubrilović, Vasa. *Iseljavanje Arnauta* [The Expulsion of the Albanians]. Manuscript in the Institute of Military History of the Yugoslav People's Army (Vojno Istorijski Institut JNA). Archives of the former Yugoslav Army (Arhiv Bivše Jugoslovenske Vojske), Belgrade, 7 March 1937. No. 2, Fasc. 4, Box 69. 19 pp.

——. *Manjinski problem u novoj Jugoslaviji.* Typescript. Belgrade, 3 November 1944. 22 pp.

——. "The Expulsion of the Albanians: Memorandum, 1937." In *Gathering Clouds: The Roots of Ethnic Cleansing in Kosovo and Macedonia. Early Twentieth-Century Documents.* Compiled, translated and edited by Robert Elsie. Dukagjini Balkan Books. Peja: Dukagjini, 2002. pp. 97-130.

——. "The Minority Problem on the New Yugoslavia: Memorandum, 1944." In *Gathering Clouds: The Roots of Ethnic Cleansing in Kosovo and Macedonia. Early Twentieth-Century Documents.* Compiled, translated and edited by Robert Elsie. Dukagjini Balkan Books. Peja: Dukagjini, 2002. pp. 149-170.

Culaj, Lush. *Komiteti Mbrojtja Kombëtare e Kosovës, 1918-1924* [National Defense Committee of Kosovo, 1918-1924]. Prishtina: Instituti Albanologjik, 1997. 252 pp.

Dedijer, Vladimir. *Jugoslovansko-albanski odnosi, 1939-1948* [Yugoslav-Albanian Relations, 1939-1948]. Na podlagi uradnih dokumentov, pisem in drugega gradiva publikacijo ured. i obdel. Ljubljana: Borba, 1949. 145 pp.

——. *Jugoslovensko-albanski odnosi, 1939-1948* [Yugoslav-Albanian Relations, 1939-1948]. Na osnovu službenih dokumenta, pisama i drugog materijala. Zagreb: Borba, 1949. 225 pp.

——. *Il sangue tradito: relazioni jugoslavo-albanesi 1938-49. Documenti ufficiali, lettere, fotografie* [Betrayed Blood: Yugoslav-Albanian Relations, 1938-1949. Official Documents, Letters, Photographs]. Milan: Editoriale periodici italiani, 1949. 221 pp.

Dogo, Marco. *Kosovo: albanesi e serbi. Le radici del conflitto* [Kosovo: Albanians and Serbs. The Roots of the Conflict]. Lungro di Cosenza, Marco 1992. v + 375 pp.

Dragnich, Alex N. *Serbia, Nikola Pašić and Yugoslavia.* New Brunswick N.J.: Rutgers University Press, 1974. 266 pp.

——. *The first Yugoslavia: Search for a Viable Political System.* Stanford: Hoover Institution Press, 1983. 182 pp.

————. *Yugoslavia's Disintegration and the Struggle for Truth.* East European Monographs, 436. Boulder: East European Monographs, 1995. xii + 278 pp.

Duka, Valentina. *Historia e Shqipërisë, 1912-2000* [History of Albania, 1912-2000]. Tirana: Kristalina KH, 2007. 559 pp.

Durham, Mary Edith. *Through the Lands of the Serb.* London: Edward Arnold, 1904. 345 pp.

————. *The Burden of the Balkans.* London: Edward Arnold, 1905. 331 pp.

————. *High Albania.* London: Edward Arnold, 1909, reprints 1970, 1985, 2000. 352 pp.

————. *The Struggle for Scutari. Turk, Slav and Albanian.* London: Edward Arnold, 1914. 320 pp.

————. *Twenty Years of Balkan Tangle.* London: George Allen & Unwin, 1920. 295 pp.

————. *Die slawische Gefahr: Zwanzig Jahre Balkan-Erinnerungen* [The Slav Peril: Twenty Years of Balkan Memories]. Deutsch herausgegeben von Hermann Lutz. Stuttgart: Robert Lutz, s.a. 356 pp.

————. *Venti anni di groviglio balcanico* [Twenty Years of Balkan Tangle]. Tradotto da Stefania Pelli-Bossi. Florence: F. Le Monnier, 1923. 341 pp.

————. *Njëzet vjet ngatëresa ballkanike* [Twenty Years of Balkan Tangle]. Shqipëruar nga inglishtia prej S. Toto. Tirana: Mesagjeritë shqiptare, 1944. 289 pp.

————. *Brenga e Ballkanit dhe vepra të tjera për Shqipërinë dhe Shqiptarët* [The Sorrows of the Balkans and Other Works about Albania and the Albanians]. Tirana: 8 Nëntori, 1990. 586 pp.

————. *Albania and the Albanians: Selected Articles and Letters, 1903-1944.* Introduction by Harry Hodgkinson. Edited by

Bejtullah Destani. London: Centre for Albanian Studies, 2001. 261 pp.

———. *The Blaze in the Balkans: Selected Writings, 1903-1941.* Edited by Robert Elsie and Bejtullah Destani, and with an introduction by Elizabeth Gowing. London, I. B. Tauris in association with The Centre for Albanian Studies, 2014. xv + 214 pp.

Dželetović Ivanov, Pavle. *21. SS Divizija Skenderbeg* [The 21st SS Scanderbeg Division]. Belgrade; Nova Knjiga, 1987. 277 pp.

———. *Jevreji Kosova i Metohije* [The Jews of Kosovo and Metohija]. Belgrade: Panpublik, 1988. 208 pp.

Elsie, Robert. "Kosovo and the Bar Tragedy of March 1945." in: *Südost-Forschungen*, Munich, 71 (2012), p. 390-400.

Ercole, Francesco (ed.). *Le terre albanesi redente 1: Cossovo* [The Redeemed Albanian Territories, 1: Kosovo]. Rome: Reale Accademia d'Italia, 1942. 280 pp.

Folić, Milutin (= Foliq, Milutin). *Komunistička Partija Jugoslavije na Kosovu, 1919-1941* [The Yugoslav Communist Party in Kosovo, 1919-1941]. Prishtina: Jedinstvo, 1987. xi + 441 pp.

———. *Partia komuniste e Jugosllavisë në Kosovë, 1919-1941* [The Yugoslav Communist Party in Kosovo, 1919-1941]. Prishtina: Rilindja, 1987. 466 pp.

Freundlich, Leo Alexander. *Albaniens Golgatha: Anklageakten wider die Vernichter des Albanervolkes* [Albania's Golgotha: Indictment of the Exterminators of the Albanian People]. Vienna: Roller, 1913. 32 pp.

———. *Golgota dell'Albania* [Albania's Golgotha]. Vicenza: Giovanni Galla, 1913. 99 pp.

———. "Albania's Golgotha: Indictment of the Exterminators of the Albanian People." In *Gathering Clouds: The Roots of*

Ethnic Cleansing in Kosovo and Macedonia. Early Twentieth-Century Documents. Compiled, translated and edited by Robert Elsie. Dukagjini Balkan Books. Peja: Dukagjini, 2002. pp. 11-46.

――――. *Die Albanische Korrespondenz: Agenturmeldungen aus Krisenzeiten (Juni 1913 bis August 1914)* [The Albanian Correspondence: News Agency Reports from a Period of Crisis (June 1913 to August 1914)]. Herausgegeben von Robert Elsie, mit einer Einleitung von Roswitha Strommer. Südosteuropäische Arbeiten, Bd. 144. Munich: Oldenbourg Verlag, 2012. lxvii + 614 pp.

Gersin, K. (= Županić, Niko). *Altserbien und die albanesische Frage* [Old Serbia and the Albanian Question]. Vienna: Anzengruber, 1912. 55 pp.

Glenny, Misha. *The Fall of Yugoslavia: The Third Balkan War.* London: Penguin, 1992. 208 pp.

Gočev, Janko Georgiev *Kosovskata operacija na bălgarskata armija prez 1915 g.* [The Kosovo Operation in the Bulgarian Army during the Year 1915]. Khaskovo: Gočev, Komereks, 2003. 78 pp.

Hadri, Ali. *Gjakova në lëvizjen nacionalçlirimtare* [Gjakova in the National Liberation Movement]. Prishtina 1974.

――――. *Këshillat nacionalçlirimtare në Kosovë, 1941-1945* [The National Liberation Councils in Kosovo, 1941-1945]. Prishtina: Enti i historisë së Kosovës, 1974. 207 pp.

――――. *Narodno-oslobodilački odbori na Kosovu, 1941-1945* [The National Liberation Councils in Kosovo, 1941-1945]. Prishtina: Zavod za istoriju Kosova, 1975. 154 pp.

Hadži-Vasiljević, Jovan. *Dodatak ratniku za januar 1909: arbanaska liga, arnautska kongra, i srpski narod u turskom carstvu, 1878-1882* [Military Supplement for January 1909: The Albanian League, the Albanian Congress and the Serbian

People under Turkish Rule, 1878-1882]. Belgrade: Srbija, 1909. iv + 127 pp.

———. *Južna Stara Srbija: istorijska, etnografska i politička istraživanja* [Southern Old Serbia: Historical, Ethnographic and Political Research]. Belgrade: Davidović, 1909, 1913. 558, 460 pp.

———. *Muslimani naše krvi u južnoj Serbiji* [Muslims of Our Blood in Southern Serbia]. Belgrade: Sv. Sava, 1924, reprint 1995. 79 pp.

———. *Arnauti naše krvi: Arnautaši* [Albanians of Our Blood]. Belgrade: Drag. Popović, 1939. 39 pp.

Hall, Richard C. *The Balkan Wars 1912-1913: Prelude to the First World War.* London: Routledge, 2000. 176 pp.

Haxhija, Sulejman. *Flamurtari i Kosovës, Isa Buletini* [Flagbearer of Kosovo: Isa Boletini]. Munich: s.e., 1967. 155 pp.

Haxhiu, Ajet. *Hasan Prishtina dhe lëvizja patriotike e Kosovës* [Hasan Prishtina and the Patriotic Movement of Kosovo]. Tirana: Naim Frashëri, 1964. 231 pp.

———. *Shota dhe Azem Galica* [Shota and Azem Galica]. Tirana: 8 Nëntori, 1976. 282 pp.

Hoti, Izber. *Çështja e Kosovës gjatë luftës së dytë botërore* [The Kosovo Question during the Second World War]. Prishtina: Qendra për Informim e Kosovës, 1997. 111 pp.

———. *Forcat e armatosura në Kosovë gjatë luftës së dytë botërore* [The Armed Forces in Kosovo during the Second World War]. Prishtina: Instituti i Historisë, 1998. 199 + xix pp.

———. *Të dhëna të panjohura për luftën e Dytë Botrore në Kosovë, 1941-1945* [Unknown Facts about the Second World War in Kosovo, 1941-1945]. Prishtina: Instituti i Historisë, 1999. 247 pp.

Hrabak, Bogumil. *Arbanaški upadi i pobune na Kosovu i u Makedoniji od kraja 1912. do kraja 1915. godine* [Albanian Invasions and Insurrections in Kosovo and Metohija from 1912 to the End of 1915]. Nacionalno nerazvijeni i nejedinstveni Arbanasi kao orude u rukama zainteresovanih država. Vranje: Narodni muzej u Vranju, 1988. 237 pp.

Human Rights Watch (ed.). *Nën pushtetin e urdhrave: krimet e luftës në Kosovë* [Under Orders: War Crimes in Kosovo]. Përktheu nga origjinali anglisht Mustafa Nano, Virgjil Muçi. Tirana: Korbi, 2002. 635 pp.

———. *Under Orders: War Crimes in Kosovo.* New York: Human Rights Watch, 2003. 593 pp.

Islami, Hivzi. *Spastrimet etnike: politika gjenocidale serbe ndaj shqiptarëve* (Ethnic Cleansings: Serb Policies of Genocide against the Albanians). Peja: Dukagjini, 2003. 389 pp.

Jelavich, Charles, and Barbara Jelavich. *The Establishment of the Balkan National States, 1804-1920.* Seattle: University of Washington Press, 1977, reprint 1986. 358 pp.

Judah, Tim. *The Serbs: History, Myth and the Destruction of Yugoslavia.* New Haven: Yale University Press, 1997. 350 pp.

Keçmezi-Basha, Sabile. *Lëvizja ilegale patriotike shqiptare në Kosovë, 1945-1947* [The Underground Albanian Patriotic Movement in Kosovo, 1945-1947]. Prishtina: Rilindja, 1998. 303 pp.

Kennan, George F. (ed.). *The Other Balkan Wars. A 1913 Carnegie Foundation Inquiry in Retrospect with a New Introduction and Reflections on the Present Conflict.* International Commission to Enquire into the Causes and Conduct of the Balkan Wars. Washington, D.C.: Carnegie Endowment for International Peace, 1993. 413 pp.

Kola, Paulin. *The Search for Greater Albania.* London: C. Hurst, 2003. xxii + 416 pp.

Krizman, Bogdan. "Elaborat Ive Andrića o Albaniji iz 1939 godine" [Draft of Ivo Andrić on Albania from the Year 1939], in *Časopis za suvremenu povijest,* Zagreb, 9 (1977), 2. pp. 77-89.

Krstić, Djordje (= Kërstiq, Gjorgje). *Kolonizacija u južnoj Srbiji* [The Colonization of Southern Serbia]. Sarajevo: Bosanka Pošta, 1928. 102 pp.

———. *Kolonizimi i Serbisë jugore: gjendja e shqiptarëve në Jugosllavi* [The Colonization of Southern Serbia: The Situation of the Albanians in Yugoslavia]. Tirana: Koha, 1994. 96 pp.

Krulic, Joseph. *Histoire de la Yougoslavie de 1945 à nos jours* [History of Yugoslavia from 1945 to the Present]. Brussels: Complexe, 1993. 256 pp.

Lalaj, Ana. *Kosova: rruga e gjatë drejt vetëvendosjes, 1948-1981* [Kosovo: The Long Road to Self-Determination, 1948-1981]. Tirana: Mësonjëtorja e parë, 2000. 434 pp.

Löhr, Hanns Christian. *Die albanische Frage: Konferenzdiplomatie und Nationalstaatsbildung im Vorfeld des Ersten Weltkrieges unter besonderer Berücksichtigung der deutschen Außenpolitik* [The Albanian Question: Conference Diplomacy and the Creation of National States Prior to the First World War, in Particular German Foreign Policy]. Inauguraldissertation zur Erlangung der Doktorwürde. Vorgelegt der Philosophischen Fakultät der Rheinischen Friedrich-Wilhelms Universität zu Bonn. Bonn, 1992. 364 pp.

Lukač, Dušan *Radnički pokret u Jugoslaviji i nacionalno pitanje, 1918-1941* [The Labor Movement in Yugoslavia and the National Question, 1918-1941]. Institut za savremeju istoriju. Belgrade: NIP Export-Press, 1972. 421 pp,

Malcolm, Noel. *Kosovo, a Short History*. London: Macmillan, 1998. 491 pp.

——. *Kosova, një histori e shkurtër* [Kosovo: A Short History]. Përkth. A. Karjagdiu. Prishtina: Koha, 1998. 506 pp.

——. *Kosovo: kratka povijest* [Kosovo: A Short History]. Sarajevo: Dani, 2000.

Milatović, Arso. *Pet diplomatskih misija* [Five Diplomatic Missions], Ljubljana and Zagreb: Cankarjeva zal. 1986) 2 vol.

——. *Kosmet, 1935-1945: moje svedočenje* [Kosmet, 1935-1945: My Testimony]. Belgrade: Naučna knjiga, 1990. 503 pp.

Milazzo, Matteo J. *The Chetnik Movement and the Yugoslav Resistance*. Baltimore: Hopkins University Press, 1975. ix + 208 pp.

Mitrović, Andrej. *Srbi i Albanci u XX veku: ciklus predavanja 7-10. maj 1990* [Serbs and Albanians in the Twentieth Century: Cycle of Lectures, 7-10 May 1990]. Belgrade: Srpska Akademija Nauka i Umetnosti, 1991. viii + 457 pp.

Murzaku, Thoma. *Politika e Serbisë kundrejt Shqipërisë gjatë luftës ballkanike, 1912-1913* [The Policies of Serbia towards Albania during the Balkan War, 1912-1913]. Tirana: Akademia e Shkencave, 1987. 416 pp.

Nasi, Lefter. *Ripushtimi i Kosovës: shtator 1944-Korrik 1945* [The Reoccupation of Kosovo, September 1944-July 1945]. Tirana: Akademia e Shkencave, 1994. 236 pp.

——. *Aspekte të shtypjes kombëtare e politike të shqiptarëve në Kosovë, 1981-1986* [Aspects of the National and Political Press of the Albanians in Kosovo, 1981-1986]. Tirana: Dardania, 1995. 147 pp.

Nedić, M. C. Gen. *Srpska vojska na albanskoj Golgoti* [The Serb Army on the Albanian Golgotha]. Belgrade: Štamparska radnica Min. Voj. I Mornarice, 1937. vi + 310 pp.

111

Nikolić, Miodrag. *Revolucionarni radički pokret na Kosovu i Metohiji, 1895-1922* [The Revolutionary Workers' Movement in Kosovo and Metohija, 1895-1922]. Prishtina: Izd. Istorijske Komisije Oblasnog Komiteta Saveza Komunista Serbije za Kosovo i Metohiju, 1962. 204 pp.

Obradović, Milovan. *Agrarna reforma i kolonizacija na Kosovu, 1918-1941* [Agrarian Reform and the Colonization of Kosovo, 1918-1941]. Prishtina: Institut za istoriju Kosova, 1981. 357 pp.

Pavlowitsch, Stevan K. *The Improbable Survivor: Yugoslavia and Its Problems, 1918-1988.* London: C. Hurst, 1988. 167 pp.

———. *Hitler's New Disorder: The Second World War in Yugoslavia.* London: Hurst, 2008. 256 pp.

Perritt, Henry H. *Kosovo Liberation Army: the Inside Story of an Insurgency.* Urbana: University of Illinois Press, 2008. xi + 230 pp.

Peruničić, Branko. *Svedočanstvo o Kosovu, 1901-1913* [Testimony on Kosovo, 1901-1913]. Belgrade: Naučna knjiga, 1988. 537 pp.

———. *Zulumi aga i begova u kosovskom vilajetu, 1878-1913* [Oppression by the Agas and Beys in the Vilayet of Kosovo, 1878.1913]. Belgrade: Nova knjiga, 1989. 670 pp.

Petković, Ranko. *Yugoslav-Albanian Relations.* Translated by Zvonko Petnički, Darinka Petković. Belgrade: Review of International Affairs, 1984. 304 pp.

Pettifer, James and Miranda Vickers. *The Albanian Question: Reshaping the Balkans.* London: I.B. Tauris, 2006. 312 pp.

Pirraku, Muhamet. *Ripushtimi jugosllav i Kosovës, 1945* [The Yugoslav Reoccupation of Kosovo, 1945]. Prishtina: Diellli, 1992. 196 pp.

———. *Kalvari i shqiptarësisë së Kosovës: Tivari 1945* [The Calvary of the Kosovo Albanians: Bar 1945]. Prishtina: Instituti Albanologjik, 1993. 75 pp.

Prishtina, Hasan. *Përmbledhje dokumentash, 1908-1934* [Collection of Documents, 1908-1934]. Tirana: 8 Nëntori, 1983. 239 pp.

———. *A Brief Memoir of the Albanian Rebellion of 1912.* Translation Elizabeth Gowing. Prishtina: Rrokullia, 2010. 52 pp.

Puto, Arben. *Pavarësia shqiptare dhe diplomacia e fuqive të mëdha, 1912-1914* [Albanian Independence and the Diplomacy of the Great Powers, 1912-1914]. Tirana: 8 Nëntori, 1978. 652 pp.

———. *L'indépendance albanaise et la diplomatie des grandes puissances, 1912-1914* [Albanian Independence and the Diplomacy of the Great Powers, 1912-1914]. Tirana: 8 Nëntori, 1982. 526 pp.

———. *Çështja shqiptare në aktet ndërkombëtare të periudhës së imperializmit: përmbledhje dokumentesh me një vështrim historik* [The Albanian Question in the International Documents of the Imperialist Period: Collection of Documents with an Historical Overview]. 2 vol. Tirana: 8 Nëntori, 1984, 1987. 403 & 686 pp.

———. *La question albanaise dans les actes internationaux de l'époque impérialiste. Recueil de documents* [The Albanian Question in the International Documents of the Imperialist Period: Collection of Documents]. 2 vol. Tirana: 8 Nëntori, 1985, 1988. 403 & 697 pp.

Rahimi. Shukri. *Lufta e shqiptarëve për autonomi, 1897-1912* [The Albanian Struggle for Autonomy, 1897-1912]. Prishtina: Enti i teksteve, 1980. 242 pp.

Rajović, Radošin (= Rajoviq, Radoshin). *Autonomija Kosova: istorijsko-pravna studija* [The Autonomy of Kosovo: A Historical and Legal Study]. Belgrade: Ekonomika, 1985. 583 pp.

———. *Autonomia e Kosovës: studim historiko-juridik* [The Autonomy of Kosovo: A Historical and Legal Study]. Prishtina: Rilindja, 1987. 498 pp.

Rakić, Milan. *Konzulska pisma, 1905-1991* [Consular Letters, 1905-1991]. Belgrade: Prosveta, 1985. 409 pp.

Ramet, Sabrina Petra. *Nationalism and Federalism in Yugoslavia, 1962-1991.* 2nd edition. Bloomington: Indiana University Press, 1992. xviii + 346 pp.

———. *Balkan Babel: The Disintegration of Yugoslavia from the Death of Tito to the War for Kosovo.* Boulder: Westview 1999. xxii + 374 pp.

———. *Balkan Babel: the Disintegration from the Death of Tito to the Fall of Milošević.* Boulder: Westview 2002. 426 pp.

———. *The Three Yugoslavias: State-Building and Legitimation, 1918-2004.* Bloomington: Indiana University Press, 2006. 784 pp.

Ratkoceri, Gani Demir. *Idriz Seferi dhe lëvizja kombëtare në Kosovën Juglindore* [Idriz Seferi and the National Movement in Southeastern Kosovo]. Tirana: s.e., 2000. 359 pp.

Ratković, Borislav. *Oslobodjenje Kosova i Metohije, 1912* [The Liberation of Kosovo and Metohija, 1912]. Belgrade: Tetra, 1997. 333 pp.

Rexhepi, Fehmi. *Gjilani me rrethinë gjatë luftës së dytë botërore, 1941-1945* [Gjilan and the Surrounding Area during the Second World War, 1941-1945]. Prishtina: Instituti i historisë, 1998. 319 pp.

Rizaj, Skënder. *Burime turke (osmane) mbi luftën e shqiptarëve për pavarësi dhe humbja e Ballkanit, 1908-1912/The Turkish (Ottoman) Sources about the Albanians' War for Independence and the Loss of the Balkans, 1908-1912*. Libri III. Prishtina & Istanbul: Akademia e Intelektualëve Shqiptarë e Shkencave dhe e Arteve, 1993. 300 pp.

Rushiti, Liman. *Lëvizja kaçake në Kosovë, 1918-1928* [The Kaçak Movement in Kosovo, 1918-1929]. Prishtina: Instituti i Historisë së Kosovës, 1981. 278 pp.

――. *Rrethanat politiko-shoqërore në Kosovë, 1912-1918* [Political and Social Relations in Kosovo, 1912-1918]. Prishtina: Rilindja, 1986. 214 pp.

――. *Kujtime për lëvizjen kaçake* [Memoirs of the Kaçak Movement]. Prishtina: s.e., 2003. 329 pp.

Rusinow, Dennison Ivan. *The Yugoslav Experiment, 1948-1974*. Royal Institute of International Affairs. London: C. Hurst, 1977. xxi + 410 pp.

Rusinow, Dennison Ivan (ed.). *Yugoslavia: A Fractured Federalism*. Washington: Wilson Center Press, 1988. 182 pp.

Shala, Xheladin. *Marrëdhëniet shqiptaro-serbe, 1912-1918* [Albanian-Serb Relations, 1912-1918]. Prishtina. Instituti Albanologjik, 1990. 367 pp.

Shehu, Ferit, and Sevdije Shehu. *Pastrimet etnike të trojeve shqiptare, 1953-1957* [The Ethnic Cleansing of Albanian Territory, 1953-1957]. Prishtina: Shoqata për Kthimin e Shqiptarëve të Shpërngulur nga Trojet e Veta, 1993. 418 pp.

Singleton, Frederick. *Twentieth-Century Yugoslavia*. London: MacMillan, 1976. 346 pp.

Stoyadinovitch, Milan. *La Yougoslavie entre les deux guerres: ni le pacte, ni la guerre* [Yugoslavia between the Two Wars: Neither Pact Nor War]. Paris: Éd. Latines, 1979. 345 pp.

115

Tautović, Radojica. *Tucović i Kosovo: eseji i polemike* [Tucović and Kosovo: Essays and Polemics]. Belgrade: Centar, 1988. 91 pp.

Tomasevich, Jozo. *The Chetniks: War and Revolution in Yugoslavia, 1941-1945.* Stanford: Stanford University Press, 1975. x + 508 pp.

Tomić, Jovan N. (= Tomitch, Yovan). *Les Albanais en Vieille-Serbie et dans le Sandjak de Novi Bazar* [The Albanians in Old Serbia and in the Sandjak of Novi Pazar]. Paris: Hachette, 1913. 86 pp.

——. *Austro-Bugarska i arbansko pitanje* [Austria, Bulgaria and the Albanian Question]. Belgrade: Kon, 1913. 160 pp.

——. *Rat na Kosovu i Staroj Srbiji 1912 godine* [War in Kosovo and Old Serbia in 1912]. Novi Sad: Električna štamparija dra Svetozara Miletića, 1913, reprint 1988. 199 pp.

Trotsky, Leon. *The Balkan Wars, 1912-1913.* New York: Monad, 1980. xxii + 524 pp.

Tucović, Dimitrije. *Srbija e Arbanija: jedan prilog kritici zavojevačke politike srpske buržoazije* [Serbia and Albania: A Contribution to the Criticism of the Aggressive Policies of the Serb Bourgeoisie]. Belgrade: Sava Radenković i brata, 1914, reprint 1974. 118 pp.

——. *Sërbia e Shqipëria, një kontribut për kritikën e politikës pushtuese të borgjezisë sërbe* [Serbia and Albania: A Contribution to the Criticism of the Aggressive Policies of the Serb Bourgeoisie]. Prishtina: Rilindja, 1975. 118 pp.

Umilta, Carlo. *Jugoslavia e Albania: memorie di un diplomatico* [Yugoslavia and Albania: Memoirs of a Diplomat]. Milan: Garzanti, 1947. vii + 201 pp.

Verli, Marenglen. *Shqipëria dhe Kosova: historia e një aspirate* [Albania and Kosovo: History of an Aspiration]. 2 vol. Tirana: Botimpex, 2007. 431 + 479 pp.

Recent Books Published in the Series "Albanian Studies," Edited by Robert Elsie

Volume 1
Tajar Zavalani, *History of Albania*. Albanian Studies, Vol. 1. London: Centre for Albanian Studies, 2015. ISBN 978-1507595671. 356 pp.

Volume 2
Robert Elsie, *Albanian Folktales and Legends*. Albanian Studies, Vol. 2. London: Centre for Albanian Studies, 2015. ISBN 978-1507631300. 188 pp.

Volume 3
Robert Elsie, *The Albanian Treason Trial (1945)*. Albanian Studies, Vol. 3. London: Centre for Albanian Studies, 2015. ISBN 978-1507709511. 347 pp.

Volume 4
Robert Elsie, *Gathering Clouds: The Roots of Ethnic Cleansing in Kosovo and Macedonia – Early Twentieth-Century Documents*. Second expanded edition. Albanian Studies, Vol. 4. London: Centre for Albanian Studies, 2015. ISBN 978-1507882085. 245 pp.

Volume 5
Robert Elsie, *Tales from Old Shkodra: Early Albanian Short Stories*. Second edition. Albanian Studies, Vol. 5. London: Centre for Albanian Studies, 2015. ISBN 978-1508417224. 178 pp.

Volume 6
Robert Elsie, *Kosovo in a Nutshell: A Brief History and Chronology of Events*. Albanian Studies, Vol. 6. London: Centre for Albanian Studies, 2015. ISBN 978-1508496748. 120 pp.

Volume 7
Robert Elsie, *Albania in a Nutshell: A Brief History and Chronology of Events*. Albanian Studies, Vol. 7. London: Centre for Albanian Studies, 2015. ISBN 978-1508511946. 93 pp.

Volume 8
Migjeni, *Under the Banners of Melancholy. Collected Literary Works*. Translated from the Albanian by Robert Elsie. Albanian Studies, Vol. 8. London: Centre for Albanian Studies, 2015. ISBN 978-1508675990. 159 pp.

Volume 9
Robert Elsie and Bejtullah Destani (ed.). *The Macedonian Question in the Eyes of British Journalists (1899-1919)*. Albanian Studies, Vol. 9. London: Centre for Albanian Studies, 2015. ISBN 978-1508696827. 311 pp.

Volume 10
Berit Backer. *Behind Stone Walls: Changing Household Organisation among the Albanians of Kosovo*. Edited by Robert Elsie and Antonia Young, with an introduction and photographs by Ann Christine Eek. Albanian Studies, Vol. 10. London: Centre for Albanian Studies, 2015. ISBN 978-1508747949. 328 pp.

Volume 11
Franz Baron Nopcsa, *Reisen in den Balkan. Die Lebenserinnerungen des Franz Baron Nopcsa*. Eingeleitet, herausgegeben und mit Anhang versehen von Robert Elsie. Albanian Studies, Vol. 11. London: Centre for Albanian Studies, 2015. ISBN 978-1508953050. 638 S.

Volume 12
Robert Elsie, *Handbuch zur albanischen Volkskultur: Mythologie, Religion, Volksglauben, Sitten, Gebräuche und kulturelle Besonderheiten*. Albanian Studies, Vol. 12. London: Centre for Albanian Studies, 2015. ISBN 978-1508986300. 484 S.

Volume 13
Jean-Claude Faveyrial. *Histoire de l'Albanie*. Edition établie et présentée par Robert Elsie. Albanian Studies, Vol. 13. Londres: Centre for Albanian Studies, 2015. ISBN 978-1511411301. xxiv + 530 pp.

Volume 14
Margaret Hasluck. *The Hasluck Collection of Albanian Folktales*. Edited by Robert Elsie. Albanian Studies, Vol. 14. London: Centre for Albanian Studies, 2015. ISBN 978-1512002287. 474 pp.

Volume 15
Ali Podrimja. *Who Will Slay the Wolf. Poetry from Kosovo*, edited and translated by Robert Elsie. Albanian Studies, Vol. 15. London: Centre for Albanian Studies, 2015. ISBN 978-1514100301. 163 pp.

Volume 16
Robert Elsie. *Keeping an Eye on the Albanians. Selected Writings in Albanian Studies*. Albanian Studies, Vol. 16. London: Centre for Albanian Studies, 2015. ISBN 978-1514157268. 556 pp.

Volume 17
Michael Schmidt-Neke. *Über das Land der Skipetaren: Buchbesprechungen aus 25 Jahren*. Herausgegeben von Robert Elsie. Albanian Studies. Vol. 17. London: Centre for Albanian Studies, 2015. ISBN 978-1514737705. 413 pp.

Volume 18
Robert Elsie. *Classical Albanian Literature: A Reader*. Albanian Studies, Vol. 18. London: Centre for Albanian Studies, 2015. ISBN 978-1515132769. 248 pp.

Volume 19
Edith Durham. *Twenty Years of Balkan Tangle*. Second Edition. Edited and introduced by Robert Elsie. Albanian Studies, Vol. 19. London: Centre for Albanian Studies, 2015. ISBN 978-1515310440. 253 pp.

Volume 20
Edith Durham. *High Albania*. New Edition. Edited by Robert Elsie. Albanian Studies, Vol. 20. London: Centre for Albanian Studies, 2015. ISBN 978-1516996766. forthcoming.

Volume 21
Edith Durham. *The Burden of the Balkans*. Second Edition. Edited by Robert Elsie. Albanian Studies, Vol. 21. London: Centre for Albanian Studies, 2015. ISBN. forthcoming.

Made in the USA
Middletown, DE
22 November 2017